Issues At The Borders of Life

edited by Bernadette Richards and Vic Pfitzner

Adelaide
2010

Interface: A Forum for Theology in the World

Volume 13, Number 1&2 2010

Interface is an ecumenical and interdisciplinary theological journal dealing with issues of a social and cultural nature.
Interface is an independently refereed journal.

Mailing address:
Interface, PO Box 504, Hindmarsh, SA 5007
email: hdregan@atf.org.au
ATF Home Page: www.atf.org.au

Subscription Rates (2010)
Australia: Individual and institutions Aus $53 p/a (includes GST)
Overseas: Individual and institutions Aus $82 p/a
Institutional Aus $88 p/a
Send all subscriptions to:
Interface
PO Box 504
Hindmarsh SA 5007

Interface is published by the ATF Theology an imprint of ATF (Australia)Ltd (ABN 90 116 359 963) and is published in May and October of each year.
Interface is indexed in the *Australasian Religion Index*
ISSN 1329-6264

Table of Contents

Interface Vol 13 1&2/2010

Introduction: On the Borders

Drew Carter and Annette Braunack-Mayer

Drew Carter
Annette Braunack-Mayer
University of Adelaide
Adelaide, Australia

All of these essays have at their core nothing less than, to quote Greg Pike, 'different conceptions of human life itself and of our place in the natural order'. Most are written, often explicitly, in response to a philosophical and broader cultural development in which the sanctity or value of all human life has been openly challenged. In recent decades such value has sometimes been acknowledged only in those possessing certain qualities such as self-awareness or the capacity to choose and then follow a direction in life. These qualities can come most under pressure at the borders of life.

Medical advances have sharpened all of the ethical 'issues at the beginning of life' that the first four essays address. In turn, they examine ethical dimensions of abortion, contraception, the use and manipulation of embryos in reproductive technology and medical research, and the legal and other debates surrounding unintended births and the arguably culpable negligence that contributed to them.

The collection ends with four essays that examine ethical dimensions of palliative care and speak to renewed pushes to legalise euthanasia and physician-assisted suicide (with the exception of Gerald Gleeson, who instead asks an underlying question).

Gareth Jones resists the conventional polarisation of the abortion debate: views can be far more nuanced and equivocal than the diametrical opposition of pro-life with pro-choice can allow. Jones diagnoses as intractable the conflict between rigid 'foetal-based' and 'mother-based' 'systems of thought': each tends to trivialise the claims of the entity that the other asserts as centrally valuable. Consequently, each system tends not to register the depth of the 'awful dilemma' (to abort or not to abort). Each resolves the dilemma one-sidedly – unhesitantly, unremittingly and universally (at least in theory). Furthermore, each system is all the weaker for being one, in the sense that what is centrally important in making decisions about abortion is not any cascade of *logic*. Logic can accord a two-celled embryo the same value as an adult human being or, conversely, lead from abortion to questioning the value of other 'non-persons' as diverse as infants, the comatose, and the severely handicapped. In both cases logic increasingly runs counter to our everyday moral experience. Rather, what is most important in making decisions about abortion is *the value actually bestowed* upon human life, as glimpsed in all manner of instructive circumstances, both pre- and postnatal.

Jones offers 'an alternative' to the polarised systems of pro-life and pro-choice. It is one guided by his interpretation of 'the Christian ethos', which carries a 'bias' against abortion by 'sensitising' us 'towards all forms of human life'. He argues against the idea that, ethically, the foetus is *completely* inviolable: this idea is not implicit in the Bible, nor is it supported by appeal to a special innocence belonging to the foetus. Foetuses are only as innocent as infants and others who participate in an imperfect world and whose claims we must balance in sometimes terrible circumstances. Jones does warn, however, against interpreting high rates of natural pregnancy loss as implicit commentary on the lesser value of foetuses. (Greg Pike echoes this warning later in the collection.) The foetus is *protectable*, not inviolable. Its claim to protection is grounded in its potential to realise its humanity (or personhood – Jones intentionally, if implicitly, collapses this distinction, as does Pike). The claim to protection is made when potential first arises – at fertilisation. Moreover, it grows in line with the foetus itself, as it develops biologically. Jones points to our usual moral responses and gives them normative weight: 'under most circumstances, the loss of a child that almost made it is felt much more acutely than that of a child that had hardly begun to develop'. He concludes with a series of 'propositions' that articulate his position:

Foetal protection should be as stringent as possible, and yet it cannot be absolute . . . There are occasions . . . when the welfare of the foetus may come into conflict with the welfare of other parties, and induced abortion is justified.

Jones offers the examples of a thirteen-year-old rape victim and of a foetus with dangerous biological abnormalities.

Ea Mulligan and **Margie Ripper** present a work not in Christian bioethics but in feminist and public health ethics. While Jones observes the 'appalling excesses of liberal abortion practices', Mulligan and Ripper accent the importance of equitable and confidential access to safe and legal contraception and abortion in empowering women to manage their own health and lives. This is important for both intrinsic and extrinsic reasons. It respects women's 'autonomy', which is intrinsically valuable. Furthermore it results in positive consequences population-wide, improving the health and social well-being of women and the children they rear. Contraception and abortion are public health measures that minimise harm, in particular the harm resulting from unsafe abortion practices: 'The harm that restrictive abortion laws cause to women's health and morbidity are well documented and world trends are towards liberalising access to abortion'. Mulligan and Ripper cite work mapping the incidence of unsafe abortion practices and consider women abused or otherwise oppressed, for whom fertility control may be especially critical in gaining health and independence. They conclude that contraception and abortion are ethical whenever they result from informed, voluntary decisions. Their arguments recognisably draw on utilitarianism and principalism, where the acquisition of informed consent is critical to respect for a patient's autonomy.

With **Greg Pike** we return from 'mother-based' to 'foetal-based' discussion. His piece is a twelve-megaton blast to the complacent and the illiterate when it comes to embryo science and the history of embryo research and use. His chronicle is comprehensive, rich in detail and insight and, all the while, considerate of the reader. He catalogues a history of proliferating experimentation and research in which embryos are created then destroyed in the pursuit of knowledge. He identifies two distinct drivers behind this activity: the 'praiseworthy goal of improving health' and the less easily assessed goal of improving the species as a whole. The reader is given the sense that this research continues to varying degrees unhinged from the full communion that for the meantime Pike only implies. He reviews current embryo manipulation and use and offers provocative speculation as to likely future directions. He also discusses the uses and misuses of empirical study in evaluating the embryo's moral status.

After examining early embryo development, Pike emphasises that at fertilisation there comes into existence an entity that is new and individual, genetically distinct from its parents. Furthermore, it contains all of the genetic information necessary to organise itself and mature. In short, it is a 'self-integrating whole organism'. On this basis Pike argues that 'the embryo is a whole individual member of the human species [merely] at an immature stage of development'. He opposes the 'gradualist' view (akin to Jones's), in which the human being and corresponding moral status emerge progressively over time. Pike imputes this view to Peter Singer. Embryos may lack *personality*, but they do not thereby lack personhood. Nor, like so many other members of the human species, do they immediately express their potential, but they no less brim with it. Pike accuses Singer of confusions on these scores that lead him to distinguish persons from members of the human species. For Pike, the distinction is nefarious: embryos are fully members of the species and therein fully valuable. The moral fellowship we share with embryos is total because the genetic fellowship we share is total: 'What adults, children and infants have that makes them valued is the very same something which makes foetuses and embryos likewise valued'. For Pike that 'something' is membership of the species.

Pike concludes that human embryos are completely inviolable: they ought no more be destroyed or risked harm to than any other member of the species. In a surprising twist, he thereby precludes the vast tracts of medical research and application that he earlier rehearses (including current *in vitro* fertilisation practices), explicitly refuting utilitarian arguments in their favour.

Bernadette Richards examines well-publicised court cases in which claims of 'wrongful life' and 'wrongful birth' have failed to win financial compensation for the negligence (usually medical) that has been found to obtain. She explains that a wrongful life action is brought by a child (or its advocate) against someone for having failed to prevent them from being born, while a wrongful birth action is brought by the parents of an unintended child against those without whose negligence the child would not have been born.

Richards diagnoses the labels of wrongful birth and wrongful life as fundamentally distracting and the cause of much muddled thinking. She redirects the focus of the courts and commentators alike away from the 'diverting' and ultimately 'derailing' broader question of whether life can ever be considered worse than the alternative (death or never having been born) and towards the 'true issue' before them, namely the detriment (financial or otherwise) suffered by one person due to the wrongful (because negligent) actions of another.

Courts have denied damages out of 'a concern that life itself will be challenged or cheapened'. But it is possible that in each case an appeal simply for financial assistance or 'relief' is misheard, strategically miscast or misdirected as a condemnation of life. Richards suggests that cases for the defence may wrongly accomplish and profit by

> a legal sleight of hand: direct the attention towards the 'abhorrent' job of placing an economic value on life and the true issue of responsibility for a harm suffered at the hands of another is put to one side.

Richards uses her knowledge of court cases in Australia and overseas in order to systematically rehearse, and then dismantle, legal arguments against any awarding of damages. She concludes that

> The true loss can be found in the removal of choice, or the denial of choice . . . The life of the child is not at issue. What ought to be at issue is the autonomy of the parents.

It is that which negligence has fundamentally compromised and in the light of which damages should be awarded.

Ian Maddocks' contribution serves as a fitting and eloquent introduction to the collection's second half. It is full of observation, as its title suggests. It shows a poetic quality that is arguably a requisite for any good meditation on the 'borderland' between life and death that an individual enters when diagnosed with a potentially fatal illness:

Like the border marches of old, where warlords engaged in repeated conflict, it is a fringe region that can be dangerous, bewildering, and scary. Its unfamiliar territory is filled with new relationships with doctors and hospitals, bringing new vocabularies of diagnosis and therapy, and – often – new discomforts.

Maddocks maps this borderland on the back of twenty years of medical work in palliative care, a specialty that concentrates on 'care rather than cure, relief of discomfort rather than reversal of pathology'. Maddocks does this narratively, delineating the routes most often taken (and which we usually expend energy putting out of mind). Here even a simple, factual outline stimulates the sympathetic imagination. Maddocks's tone is humble and direct; he touches the daily reality of death 'tentatively, with a sense of awe and agnosticism'. The effect is quite moving, and as a guide he earns our trust.

His routes include a gateway (diagnosis), resistance to entry (a resolve to fight), journeying (receiving palliative care), and the question of hastening that journey (euthanasia):

> Many patients will ask about how it might be possible to hasten the inevitable . . . Usually, in my experience, this is not an ideological statement building from long-standing advocacy for euthanasia, but a response to a feeling of powerlessness, and of being a nuisance and an expense to family and society.

Maddocks registers the conflict that arises for him as a doctor: he seeks to act beneficently and to respect the patient's autonomy but also to do no harm (more formally, to obey the ethical principle of non-maleficence). In this articulation he draws on the principlist approach used also by Mulligan and Ripper. Maddocks touches on 'many complexities' and ultimately advocates 'a cautious approach', encouraging 'further consideration and debate' before any legislative change. He invites advocates of change to recognise the complexities and to be 'respectful of the wonder of life and the mystery of death' (which, we might observe, an accent on autonomy alone cannot register).

Rosalie Hudson examines palliative care within the context of end-stage dementia. She seeks to significantly reorient it, critiquing the 'traditional bio-medical paradigm' and offering in its place a ('countercultural') vision of care that is arguably more worthy of the name. The traditional bio-medical paradigm mistakes aging for 'a scientific problem ripe for a technical solution': end-stage dementia foremost calls for a certain *doing* in response. Hudson disagrees. She distinguishes questions of what we are to *do* from those of how we are to *relate* (and of what things might *mean*), not reducing ethics to the former. Hudson mines both words and relationships for their meaning. To 'palliate' originally meant to 'cloak', to protectively cover distressing symptoms. The first 'hospice' was so called by virtue of the 'true hospitality' that carers showed their charges. Hudson observes that

> the world of dementia . . . lends itself . . . to imagination and creativity, and the risky business of appearing foolish and 'non-professional' in an attempt to understand the other person's situation.

In this fragment alone we can find Hudson's emphasis. It falls less on patient management than on the *meaning* of patients' lives, of the lives that mingle with theirs, and of the relationships that develop. As human beings we exist and find meaning 'in mutuality and reciprocity—in the *interdependence* of our relationships', and this is imaged in the Holy Trinity. This anthropology contrasts with Pike's, whereby human beings are centrally defined not by their relationships but by their shared genetics. It serves the same end, however: 'When persons are seen in their communal relationships, no person can be regarded as more, or less, worthy of care than any other person'. Like Pike, Hudson opposes Singer. She considers his conception of the person to be an absurdity that threatens to kill both frail older people and (what is less commonly observed) the spirit of our relationships with them.

How are we to relate to people with end-stage dementia? Hudson answers that we should recognise our own dependency (on one another and on God) and thereby with humility care for the 'whole person', not merely what presents as the sum of their symptoms. We are equals together 'in Christ'. Even when we forget ourselves God remembers us—this is Hudson's cause for hope. God calls us to remember one another, and even *for* one another: in ministering spiritually to those with dementia, we might remember God for them. Such a vision contrasts radically with Hudson's target, which casts the dementia patient foremost as devoid of 'rationality' and 'autonomy'.

Hudson adds to her anthropology some consequentialist reinforcement: 'the therapeutic value of human-to-human encounter is incalculable'. She concludes with practical recommendations for change in both carer practice and education, and emphasises the importance of establishing comprehensive care plans with patients and their families early on.

To the question posed by his chapter title, **Gerald Gleeson** answers 'yes'. He argues that life is the most fundamental thing that is good *for* a person. It enables every other thing good for a person and, indeed, is presupposed in any (usually consequentialist) attempt at weighing goods and ills in a life. Life has (in Kant's sense) a transcendental character—Gleeson interpolates 'value'—defying reduction to but one good among many.

Life is no mere 'instrument': it ought not to be intentionally consumed in the service of a higher goal, though it may be lost as an unintended side-effect, as in martyrdom or heroism. (In this clause we can glimpse the principle of double effect that Helen McCabe soon explores.) 'Being alive is not the highest personal good'. That good resides instead in expressing and fulfilling one's nature as a being self-directed but no less responsible to 'objective parameters'. Gleeson cites Aquinas: the realisation of its nature stands as the fundamental good *of* the person (with goods *for* the person following accordingly). But so centrally necessary to fulfilling our nature is being alive that we cannot intentionally take our own lives, just as we cannot sell ourselves into slavery. (Gleeson cites Mill here.) We cannot relinquish liberty for liberty's sake, nor willingly extinguish our own wills (or opportunities for their future expression): we would undercut the very thing we hope to affirm, contradicting ourselves. Far from suicide ever crowning autonomy, it undercuts it at the root. Life cannot be forfeited in the name of autonomy, for without life there can be no (further) autonomy. Life lies at the heart, not the margins, of the good of the person: 'the most fundamental way of respecting a person, myself or others, is by respecting their life' (not necessarily their wishes).

Gleeson also implies, we think, that intentionally to 'take, control and end' life, thereby determining its final meaning, is hubristic or fat on the notion of being one's own. It denies the 'objective parameters' of human nature that make of choices good and bad ones. An act is not good simply because it is freely chosen. Gleeson cites Charles Taylor in arguing that choices presuppose 'horizons of intelligibility and value' that make them meaningful. These horizons derive from the nature of reality, Gleeson proposes.

Helen McCabe concludes the collection in defence of the principle of double effect (PDE) as applied in end-of-life decisions. She defends the distinction between intending and (merely) foreseeing, arguing against critics who see none and who accordingly wish to legalise euthanasia with the view that it already occurs in practice. She does this first by expanding on the 'ethical tradition' (recognisably Christian) in which the PDE 'finds its philosophical home', then by attempting to demonstrate its superior realism with respect to moral psychology. McCabe's tradition recognises as morally significant the intrinsic nature of an act, its intention, its motive (or animating spirit, we might suggest), and its consequences for the 'the kind of person we become'. By contrast, the 'post-traditionalists', whom McCabe trains into her sights, exalt only autonomy and (broadly practical or material) consequences. (On this front McCabe allies with Hudson and opposes Mulligan and Ripper.) McCabe sees as two inadequacies of the post-traditionalist account its equations of medical negligence with outright murder and of withholding or withdrawing life support with killing (as otherwise distinct from 'letting die'). These equations are enabled by all disregard for intention as 'morally and psychologically distinct' from the ability to foresee.

McCabe concedes that not all end-of-life decisions can be 'guided coherently' by the PDE. A resource even older to McCabe's tradition may be needed, namely the distinction between ordinary and extraordinary measures of care. If a treatment represents something too extraordinary to ask of a patient, too painful, inaccessible, denigrating, repugnant, or morally or spiritually violative a recourse, then the patient may morally forego it.

McCabe concludes with some reflection on human dignity and on multiple threats to it posed by post-traditionalists. In particular she considers frightening any reduction of doctors to mere technicians in the service of our (ever vulnerable and variable) wills.

What are we to conclude from these rich and complex accounts of beginnings and ends in life? As noted at the outset, all of these accounts are concerned to enrich how we conceptualise human life. And yet, despite this, they both cut past and illuminate each other. There is a disconnectedness about these essays, a sense in which some of their writers seem to live and work in countries that are far removed from and foreign to one another. They just 'do things differently'.[1] This is most obvious if one compares the epistemology, ontology and sometimes theology that can be glimpsed (or guessed at) in various accounts. Differences on these counts can (but do not always) correspond to how central autonomy is taken to be in defining both morality and our very humanity (or personhood). Mulligan and Ripper and Richards would seem to assign autonomy a fundamental importance that Hudson, Gleeson and McCabe openly contest. Jones, Pike and Maddocks are perhaps border watchers or riders here, negotiating the concept in ways that traverse or avoid divides. Could any be bridged by more work toward a theological conception of autonomy, or of what that concept hopes to preserve and promote?

While these essays challenge our capacity to successfully integrate their ideas, they simultaneously enhance our understanding of them. Reading the essays as a collection rather than as individual rhetorical pieces, one

1. Leslie P Hartley, *The Go-Between*, 1953.

can see how questions on some points are clarified by insights on others. For example, there exists a common thread of concern for human dignity, whether that be expressed through a desire to protect the vulnerable or to respect autonomous choices. Perhaps an adequate account of human dignity must unite both of these strands. There is also room for readers to align with that tradition which best expresses their own values while simultaneously being challenged to explore the limits of those values. The title of the collection thus bears on both the borders of human life and our own ethical borders, and these essays succeed in examining both.

Interface Vol 13 1&2/2010

Abortion: An Alternative to the Conflict Paradigm

D Gareth Jones

Gareth Jones
University of Otago
Dunedin, New Zealand

Attitudes in conflict

I am approaching the issue of abortion from a bioethical perspective rather than a legal one. I am also writing as one who has considerable interests in closely related bioethical issues, namely, the artificial reproductive technologies (ARTs). Both abortion and the ARTs are concerned with prenatal human life, albeit with the foetus and embryo respectively. Approaches to abortion have had considerable implications for debate on the ARTs, since many commentators recognise little distinction between the foetus and embryo. In my view, this has proved misleading and unhelpful for discussion of embryo research and embryonic stem cells,[1] and so it behoves us to deal in a judicious manner with abortion.

For many, the only legitimate approach to the abortion issue is one expressed in terms of a *conflict paradigm*. According to this view, there are only two perspectives on abortion and these are locked in mortal combat. We can sum up these perspectives, seen in essentially simple terms, with the epithets 'pro-life'[2] and 'pro-choice', although 'anti-abortion' and 'pro-

1. D Gareth Jones, 'Responses to the human embryo and embryonic stem cells: Scientific and theological assessments', *Science and Christian Belief*, 17 (2005): 199–222.
2. The term 'right-to-life' is commonly used. This presupposes an ethical approach based on rights, according to which all individuals have a series of rights. From a Christian

abortion' are equally apt. In other words, the vast complexity of moral discourse is whittled down to a simple decision—either an absolute stance in favour of the unborn or an absolute stance in favour of the mother's right to self-determination. It is the one *or* the other, so that any mediating position is automatically placed in one or other of these categories. Consequently, any position that allows just one abortion (except where the mother's physical life is, or may be, placed in jeopardy) is regarded (by pro-life advocates) as pro-choice, while any position that places restrictions upon the mother's freedom of choice is regarded (by pro-choice advocates) as pro-life.

The end-result of such attitudes is that the pro-life group treats advocates of a relatively conservative, non-absolutist position as if they were promulgating abortion on demand. In precisely the same way, the pro-choice group regards them as advocates of the most doctrinaire pro-life sentiments.

One of the major consequences of this conflict paradigm is that the abortion debate is carried out entirely in terms of competing *systems of thought*. These can be resolved into a foetal based system and a mother based system. If the foetal based system is adopted, all considerations relevant to the mother or family are relegated so that the foetus becomes the sole object of moral attention. In the extreme versions of this approach, one is tempted to conclude that greater value is bestowed upon foetal life than upon postnatal life. The opposite holds when the mother based system is used as the basis of ethical decision making, since in that situation the mother's concerns completely overrule any foetal concerns.

The attraction of logical arguments

Although these two systems are mutually exclusive, their approach has much in common. Implicit within both is a driving force grounded in *logical argument*. The foetal-based system, with its legitimate concerns for the welfare of the foetus, is driven to view the two-celled embryo in precisely the same ethical terms as the three-month-old foetus, which in turn

perspective, there is the difficulty that the Bible does not speak of rights, and so it is far from clear that we always have a right to life. Further, if a foetus has a right to life, so does the mother, who may also have other rights, such as the right to decide what to do with her own body, the right to self-determination, or the right to terminate a pregnancy. When rights come into conflict, an ethical decision has to be made based on other principles.

has exactly the same status as an adult human being. Each is considered to be a human person with all the rights (if not all the obligations) of a fully developed person. The logic is exemplary. What is far from clear is whether the logical progression backwards from adult to foetus to embryo has meaning, let alone ethical compulsion, in social and theological terms. For its part, the mother-based system with its questioning of the value of the foetus leads to a questioning of the value of the infant, the comatose, the mentally handicapped, and the senile. Since the foetus is deemed a non-person, so is the infant (perhaps for the first two to three years of life) as well as various groups with severe brain damage. Here again is a logical progression, this time working in the opposite direction—from embryo to foetus to infant to adult. Again, it poses serious dilemmas for ethical decision-making, since it undermines confidence in the value of many groups of human beings.

In both instances, the logic inherent within the systems leads to conclusions that appear to be in conflict with legitimate human concerns. For instance, some commentators in arguing against the ethical legitimacy of abortion following the rape of, let us say, a thirteen-year-old girl give the impression of having little concern for the girl and her welfare. Such concern has no place in a rigid foetal-based system; arguments in favour of abortion on the ground of compassion for the girl are readily dismissed as sentimental and unethical, since they show no compassion for the foetus.[3] In making these comments, I am not suggesting that abortion is the inevitable answer in this instance, only that a foetal-based system may lead to facile solutions that ignore many genuine human dilemmas. In exactly the same way, those who lightly dismiss one-year-olds as non-persons with no claims on society and no inherent value as human beings (unless *we* bestow value on them) are well on the way to rendering all human beings disposable. The logic of such a system is irreconcilable with any tradition rooted in genuine human concern.

Excessive dependence upon the logical outworking of these systems has a further repercussion, namely, that ethical decisions are arrived at entirely by logic. Hence, proponents of a foetal based system regularly

3. Harold OJ Brown, *Death Before Birth* (Nashville: Thomas Nelson, 1977). Brown considers that compassion is a utilitarian argument, and that genuine compassion cannot ease the predicament one person must suffer at the price of destroying another. Following Baruch Brody, he argues that the life could be saved by the mother enduring several months of inconvenience, some embarrassment and social discrimination (147).

resort to the 'slippery slope' argument. This enshrines a logical necessity: abortion for genetic reasons inevitably leads to abortion for superficial social reasons, and this in turn leads to abortion on demand; abortion itself inevitably leads to infanticide, and this inevitably leads to euthanasia (both voluntary and involuntary). Such a progression overlooks the complex nature of ethical decision-making and of arriving at value judgments. There may be compelling ethical reasons for distinguishing between these actions, even if logic (or, as it has also been termed, the 'fallacy of the continuum')[4] suggests that killing in the one circumstance justifies killing in all the other circumstances. In practice, we make such distinctions in every area of daily existence. Why not also when dealing with abortion?

Foetal inviolability—its nature and consequences

I have argued in many places that the notion of foetal inviolability is not implicit within the Bible, at least not in the sense that foetal life is *completely* protectable.[5] However, what if that position were espoused? What are its bioethical repercussions?

Foetal innocence

The notion of foetal inviolability is closely associated with that of foetal innocence, since it is the latter that leads to demands for the total protection of foetuses. The difficulty with this concept is that it tends to isolate them from the conflict inherent in a far from perfect world. Foetuses are no more inviolable in practice than are postnatal humans. Both are integrally related to a world in conflict; both are destroyed and disfigured by disease, greed, envy, accidents, and by the unjust actions of individuals or societies, and selfishness.

Foetuses mirror what we *are* far more precisely than we frequently wish to admit. They are one with us in the human endeavour; they benefit by our creativity and scientific expertise, and are put at risk by our technological misadventures and short-term aspirations. As foetuses live with us, they experience the results of our faithfulness to God, but also of our rebellion against God.

---

4. This is the term used by Robert N Wennberg, *Life in the Balance* (Grand Rapids: Eerdmans, 1985), 66.
5. See the discussion of the biblical material in D Gareth Jones, *Manufacturing Humans* (Inter-Varsity Press, Leicester, 1987), chapter 5.

Foetuses are no more innocent than are infants and young children; both groups are weak and in need of protection. Moreover, both are due the profoundest respect because they are partakers with us in what it means to be human. Because of their weakness and defencelessness, we are called to place a wall of compassion and protection around them as we do around pregnant women, the physically and mentally handicapped, the aging and the senile.

When viewed like this, we begin to appreciate the appalling excesses of liberal abortion policies. We also begin to appreciate that foetuses are placed at peril by many other factors, and that foetuses themselves may place at peril other people within the human community (especially the mother). This is a manifestation of the human likeness that characterises foetuses. Thus, to regard them as 'especially' innocent is to place them out of reach of the conflict inherent in the human condition. Paradoxically, if they were not so much like us, they would not constitute such a challenge to us.

Pregnancy wastage

The query raised by the enormously high levels (fifty to seventy per cent) of pregnancy wastage (often referred to as spontaneous abortion, one of its constituents) is whether this astronomically high natural loss justifies treating foetuses as inviolable. It is unfortunate, however, that it has proved all too easy to use this natural loss of foetuses as justification for deliberately destroying normal foetuses. This is a misuse of the pregnancy wastage data, since a *natural* phenomenon should not be converted into a *moral* guideline. The existence of diseases 'in nature' is not a reason to prohibit attempts at curing them, let alone obligating us to induce them.[6]

Despite these provisos, pregnancy wastage poses a major challenge to those for whom fertilisation endows 'innocent' human lives with all the rights ascribed to persons, including a right not to be killed and a right to protection in life threatening situations. If foetuses are innocent and on these grounds should never be deliberately aborted, it follows that foetuses about to be spontaneously aborted are equally innocent. On this basis, arguments against the taking of foetal life by induced abortion should be matched by attempts to save foetal life that would otherwise be spontaneously aborted.

6. TF Murphy, 'The moral significance of spontaneous abortion', *Journal of Medical Ethics*, 11 (1985): 79–83.

A major problem with pregnancy wastage is that the cause of the wastage in fifty per cent of cases is chromosomal abnormality.[7] To attempt to save every foetus about to be spontaneously aborted would mean allowing into life an astronomically large number (perhaps 2.5 million per year in the United States) of abnormal children. While this is not feasible at present (and may never be), we have to ask whether it would be justifiable to produce handicapped life on this scale. Were we to override the 'protective mechanism' of spontaneous abortion, we would be uncovering vast sources of developmental abnormalities. It is this that makes the pregnancy wastage debate so different from efforts to decrease prenatal mortality rates, where in principle to save life is to produce healthy, normal life.

Foetuses and human conflict

Foetal life is placed in jeopardy by many circumstances— spontaneous abortion (as discussed above); the use of certain contraceptives (such as the intra-uterine device [IUD] and the morning-after pill); a scarcity of medical resources; the mother smoking cigarettes, drinking alcohol or suffering from malnutrition during pregnancy; a whole range of environmental pollutants, and war. If foetuses are to receive absolute protection from fertilisation onwards, in the sense that anyone approving of just one abortion is committing a serious moral offence, each of these actions must also be a serious moral offence. To perform an act known to carry with it a high probability (in some cases, certainty) that foetuses will be destroyed or maimed is a denial of their 'right' to life and health. Once we regard embryos and foetuses as inviolable, it follows that to use an IUD, to permit high levels of certain pollutants in the atmosphere, to allow pregnant women to smoke or to engage in warfare in which it is known that pregnant women (and therefore foetuses) will be killed, are all morally objectionable activities.

These illustrations underline the extreme difficulty of providing the foetus with absolute protection. Even if it could be done in one circumstance (such as by prohibiting induced abortion), it would be impossible to do in many other circumstances (unless IUDs, smoking and drinking during pregnancy, environmental pollution, malnutrition, and war were also prohibited). This does not mean we should welcome liberal abortion policies; on the contrary, we should oppose them. My point is that to do so on the basis of foetal inviolability is doomed to failure.

---

7. See figures given in D Gareth Jones, *Bioethics* (Adelaide: ATF Press, 2007), 66–8.

The concept of foetal inviolability implies that killing a three-day-old embryo (by using an IUD), undergoing an abortion either for serious or flippant reasons, allowing a severely handicapped child (with only a few days of prospective life) to die, killing a mother and her foetus in a 'just' war, and killing an adult in cold blood, are equally morally objectionable. While not condoning any of these actions, I can only conclude that to treat them as equivalent in moral seriousness is to render impossible any form of responsible ethical decision making. What is required are criteria that place considerable weight on the value of the foetus while allowing ethical judgments to be made between the relative merits of circumstances in which foetuses are placed in jeopardy.

Foetuses as protectable beings

In the search for alternatives to foetal inviolability, two main positions have emerged. Foetuses either warrant no protection (they are non-persons), or they warrant some protection (perhaps very considerable protection) but this is not as great as the protection given to adults.[8]

I shall ignore completely the position that foetuses deserve no protection. Although this is a seriously held ethical position, it is not usually regarded as a theological option. The other alternative is a gradualist or developmental one, whereby the foetus is to be protected at all stages of its development with the degree of protection increasing as development proceeds. This position may be stated in terms of the *potential* of the foetus: its potential for full personhood. Consequently, a three-day-old embryo is not regarded as possessing the significance of an adult (in practical terms, is this even possible?), but neither is it regarded as of no value, nor is it considered to be readily disposable. It *has* considerable value on account of its potential as a human being and as a person able to respond to other persons and to God.

According to the potentiality principle, there is no point in development, no matter how early on, when the foetus (embryo) does not display some elements of personhood, however rudimentary they may be. The potential is there, and it is for this reason that the foetus has a claim to life and profound respect. This claim, however, becomes stronger as foetal development proceeds, so that by the latter stages of gestation the claim is so

---

8. See the discussion in D Gareth Jones, *Valuing People* (Carlisle: Paternoster Press, 1999), chapter 7.

strong that the consequences of killing such a foetus are the same as those of killing an actual person—whether child or adult. Conversely, the foetus in the last trimester will, when necessary, be treated as a 'patient'. Another way of expressing this notion is to say that the principle of foetal protection is applied weakly at early stages in the person forming process and progressively more strongly as the process progresses. In other words, the reasons for harming need to get progressively stronger as foetuses come closer to being fully fledged persons.[9]

Critics of the potentiality principle invariably want a hard and fast answer concerning precisely *when* the foetus becomes protectable. Such an arbitrary line, however, is against the thrust of this principle, according to which human life is *always* deserving of protection no matter how immature it may be. What the principle does not do is allow the developing human to be viewed in complete isolation of all the other humans intimately involved with it, since all are to be treated as beings of dignity and as deserving of respect.

In ordinary life, we recognise a difference between the accidental loss of an embryo or early foetus and the birth of a stillborn child. Both entail the death of foetal life and yet, under most circumstances, the loss of a child that almost made it is felt much more acutely than that of a child that had hardly begun to develop. The potentiality principle takes account of the respective degrees of development lying behind these responses. It never underestimates the significance of even the earliest stages of embryonic and foetal growth, but it does treat with seriousness the developmental continuum of which the foetus is an integral part.

The potentiality principle never provides grounds for lightly disposing of the foetus. However, when serious discord arises between the welfare of the mother and that of the foetus she is carrying, it provides general guidance for assessing the weight given to the claims of the foetus, in so far as its degree of development is concerned. It also confers respect on the early embryo, since at no stage is the embryo a non-person and at no stage is it of no value as an end in itself. Neither the embryo nor foetus can ever be disposed of at will. According to this interpretation of the potentiality principle, its aim is to conserve foetal life.

The potentiality principle accepts that the foetus (or embryo) represents an integral stage in the future history of that particular human being/person. As such, it cannot be disposed of at will. At the same time,

9. Keith Ward, 'Persons, kinds and capacities', in Peter Byrne, editor, *Rights and Wrongs in Medicine* (London: King Edward's Hospital Fund for London, 1986), 53–79.

it concedes that the mere existence of the foetus, without any reference whatsoever to its present properties, constitutes insufficient grounds for making definitive ethical judgments when there is a clash between that foetus and another human person possessing far more of the properties of actual personhood. Consequently, the potentiality principle does not usher in rigid rules about precisely when abortion is or is not justified. What the potentiality principle does is to provide limits and guidelines. Within a Christian context, these lead to the foetus being treated with immense respect and as a being of very considerable worth in the sight of God.

The awful dilemma

The position I have arrived at can be expressed in terms of a series of propositions.

Proposition 1

Under all normal circumstances, a foetus is to be regarded as a gift of God, a gift to be accepted and incorporated into the family circle. The ideal is *always* protection of foetal life, since this is the way of non-violence, peace, and reconciliation. Consequently, what requires justification is not the protection of foetal life but abortion. The Christian ethos leads to a bias against abortion, just as it leads to a bias against the destruction and despoliation of human life in other situations. It will also ensure that we become sensitised towards all forms of human life (and not desensitised in the face of human suffering and anguish), and that we refrain from taking human life out of self-interest.

Proposition 2

Our valuation of the foetus should preclude us from accepting abortion as an ethically neutral act. It is a violation of all that the foetus stands for as a human being made by God for his own purposes and with the potential for responding to God as a moral and spiritual being. Induced abortion, by its very nature, is a process initiated by human beings, by which a human life with enormous potential is destroyed. In similar vein, spontaneous abortion also brings a human life to a premature end. It, too, lays ethical obligations upon the community.

Proposition 3

Foetal protection should be as stringent as possible, and yet it cannot be absolute. Foetuses cannot be isolated from the conflicts inherent in the human condition. Consequently, to expect complete protection for foetuses but accept less than complete protection for adults is to impose on foetuses an aura of idealism we do not impose on other members of the human community. Self-centredness, pride, arrogance, deception and lust invade the sexual side of human existence as much as any other facet of daily life, and the consequences for foetuses, children, and parents may be tragic, and may be compounded by appalling disease and grotesque deformity, which are all the more strident when present in foetuses and neonates. There are occasions, therefore, when the welfare of the foetus may come into conflict with the welfare of other parties, and induced abortion is justified. There are also many occasions when abnormalities in the developing embryo lead to spontaneous abortion.

Proposition 4

The degree of protection afforded the foetus will vary with the degree of foetal development, increasing as development proceeds. A three-month-old foetus (let alone one that is seven months old) deserves more protection than a three-day-old embryo since, in terms of the potentiality/gradualist position, the former is closer to realising full personhood than is the latter. Despite this, the three-day-old embryo has considerable value even if this is not as great as is the value of a later foetus.

Proposition 5

Foetal protection is to be abrogated only in situations where there is (or appears to be) unresolvable tension. This will usually be between mother and foetus, although it may also involve the family unit, and it may be exacerbated by serious medical circumstances afflicting the foetus or on some occasions the mother. The discord will be of sufficient severity to jeopardise the integrity of mother and/or family. This will vary widely from one situation to another, depending on the Christian convictions (or lack of them) of the parties involved, the social and religious culture in which the couple is living, and the degree of support available in the community (in terms of the social and medical services available and the help of family and friends). Circumstances may prove critical in determining whether the discord is resolvable or unresolvable.

Proposition 6

The crucial principle in assessing abortion decisions is the value placed upon human life, both pre- and postnatal. The value actually bestowed upon humans is of greater importance than theoretical systems, such as foetal inviolability. While this does not deny the significance of general guidelines, it emphasises that the way in which we treat human beings is critical. With this as our starting-point, we shall refrain from aborting foetuses except in the most extreme circumstances, even in the absence of a rigid concept of foetal inviolability. We shall act as though foetuses are 'almost inviolable', in the same way as we should treat postnatal humans as 'almost inviolable'. We shall also pay considerable attention to the value we place on the mother's welfare, and we shall be concerned for her good in relation to that of the foetus.

Proposition 7

The dilemma of abortion will not be solved by legislation, since the latter, by itself, cannot successfully counteract the appalling excesses of liberal abortion practices. This does not mean that legislative changes towards more conservative abortion legislation would not be welcome (and indeed should be contended for).

A difficulty frequently overlooked by advocates of an exceedingly restrictive legislative approach is that very many people are not persuaded that abortion is murder. Furthermore, many hold that the foetus is, at least at certain stages during its development, a non-person. These are legitimate postulates, however strongly one may disagree with one or both of them, and they are not compatible with the belief that the foetus should be given absolute protection. To attempt to enforce legislative restrictions on these people, when they have not been convinced by ethical arguments, is a tenuous way forward in a pluralist society. Neither does it have a self-evident theological base.

Interface Vol 13 1&2/2010

Ethics of Contraception and Abortion

Ea Mulligan and Margie Ripper

Ea Mulligan
Flinders University of South Australia
Adelaide, Australia
Margie Ripper
University of Adelaide
Adelaide, Australia

Abstract

Contraception and abortion are ethical when they result from informed, voluntary decisions. Fertility control services contribute to positive public health outcomes, as do education and economic independence for women. Confidential services support the ethical principle of autonomy, allowing women to take action to maximise their own health and the well-being of their dependents. The ethical principal of justice also supports access to contraception and abortion.

Access to fertility control is widely contested; however, competing claims over women's reproductive capacity do not outweigh the ethical value accorded to the autonomy of women and the benefits which flow from self-determination.

Ethics of contraception and abortion

The goals of public health include maximising self-determination, improving the health status of populations and augmenting the ability of parents to raise healthy children. Abortion and contraception are only two amongst many interventions which contribute to achieving these public health goals. The ethical considerations which public health practitioners apply to the provision of abortion and contraception include: respecting the autonomy of individuals, seeking to minimise harm, acknowledging competing interests and appreciating the fairness of providing access to health services for everyone.

The same ethical considerations underpin public health provision of both contraception and abortion. There is no clear demarcation between preventing pregnancy and intercepting pregnancy. Using ethical grounds to distinguish between abortion and contraception suggests that women who are not yet pregnant and women who are already pregnant each have a different moral status. Any distinction has become less meaningful following the widespread adoption of post-coital fertility control methods such as menstrual extraction, pharmaceutical interception of pregnancy prior to implantation, and the use of contraceptive devices which interrupt implantation but not conception. This continuum between contraception and abortion technologies highlights the need to rely on ethical principles which are applicable to both.

The Autonomy of Women

The most significant ethical considerations of fertility control centre upon the autonomy of individual women and their authority to make decisions regarding reproduction, their future and their heath care. Forced sterilisation, surreptitious contraception and compelled abortion are all unethical because each denies the autonomy of women.

Family formation, pregnancy and childbearing have an enormous impact on women's life chances. Ability to influence these events gives women the opportunity to enhance their own health and well-being. Women also seek to maximise the opportunities for the health and development of their children. For women who have very little opportunity to make decisions about their circumstances or their sexual relationships (such as those living with domestic violence, drug dependency or on the very margins of their society), fertility control may provides an opportunity to exercise self-determination and exert some influence over their future.

Respect for the autonomy of women requires their consent to all health interventions. In order to make informed decisions and provide consent, they must understand the risks of contraception, abortion and child bearing. The risks associated with each of these vary according to the health care practices and products used and the social and economic context which prevails. Providing accurate information is an ethical and often a legal obligation. In many jurisdictions with a common law tradition, medical practitioners have a duty of care and this duty includes providing warnings about the risks of treatment. Valid evidence concerning risk is required by both practitioner and patient to inform consent. There is a strong body of scientific evidence demonstrating the safety of the widely available forms of contraception as well as the safety of abortion.

Respect for autonomy also underlies the requirement for privacy. The concepts that a woman has a right to privacy and that decisions concerning abortion and contraception are private matters to be decided by a woman and her doctor were embodied in a US Supreme Court decision which established access to abortion and identified the right to privacy as a facet of the United States constitution.[1] Privacy legislation adopted by many members of the Organisation for Economic Cooperation and Development is derived from the Guidelines on the Protection of Privacy and Transborder Flows of Personal Information (1980).[2] These guidelines assert that people may control disclosure of personal information, and that they have a right of access to the records kept about them.

The right of patients to expect confidential health care has been consistently defended by medical practitioners and public health advocates. Confidentiality acknowledges the autonomy of patients by respecting their decisions about who may know their secrets. It also encourages patients to trust health providers with sensitive information, which may be important in providing care. This has long been recognised as a prerequisite for treating sexually transmitted diseases and is necessary for the provision of all sexual health services, including contraception and abortion. In particular, teenagers will not attend sexual health services if they believe their parents will discover that they are sexually active.[3]

Minimising harm

Another major ethical principle on which provision of contraception and abortion rests is the minimisation of harm to women. Two questions arise from consideration of the ethical principal of non-maleficence (do no

---

1. Roe v Wade (1973) 410 U.S. 113.
2. These guidelines may be accessed at http://www.oecd.org/document/
3. See E Mulligan and A Braunack-Mayer, 'Why protect confidentiality in health information? A review of the research evidence', in *Australian Health Review*, 28 (2004): 48–55.

harm). Is giving women decision making authority over their reproduction harmful or health enhancing to women, and is fertility control harmful or health enhancing for women?

Is self-determination harmful to women?

Public health requires attention to a wide range of factors which contribute to well-being. For women, opportunities to gain and maintain employment, participate in public life and contribute to decision making forums all enhance health. Women's social participation is restricted by many factors. Where child care is entirely the responsibility of mothers and employment conditions conflict with parental responsibilities, child rearing becomes a disability. When faced with discrimination, access to fertility control provides women with opportunities for self-development.

When contraception and abortion are accessible, women may choose to raise a smaller number of healthier children. The ability to determine family size improves women's sense of well-being irrespective of the number of children they bear. The contribution which control over family size makes to women's well-being is illustrated by research such as that conducted by Hardee and others in Indonesia.[4]

Are contraception or abortion harmful to women?

The very low risk associated with contraception or abortion conducted using safe techniques and the contrasting higher risks associated with childbirth and unsafe abortion are ethically significant. They indicate that generally available contraception is a harm minimisation strategy and legally sanctioned abortion is the least harmful pregnancy outcome.

Consideration of potential harm to women has been important in framing legislation regulating abortion in many jurisdictions. Legislation may permit abortion where the risk to the pregnant woman from abortion is less than the risk of continuing the pregnancy (all pregnancies) or, more restrictively, where there is grave risk to the life of the pregnant woman if the pregnancy continues (few pregnancies). While legislation varies in the range of circumstances in which abortion is sanctioned, the underlying

4. K Hardee, E Eggleston, E Wong Irwanto and T Hull, 'Unintended pregnancy and women's psychological well-being in Indonesia', in *Journal of Biosocial Sciences*, 36 (2004): 617–26.

ethical principle embodied in these provisions is that the life of the pregnant woman is important and she will be permitted to take action that increases her chances of survival.

Assessment of risk has concerned legislators in regulating abortion in many jurisdictions. A concern that women may not act in their own best interests when choosing abortion has led to the substitution of another decision maker (often a judicial officer or a doctor) in some jurisdictions. The substitute decision maker is then called upon to decide whether the risks of abortion are acceptable in individual cases.

Where only unsafe abortion is available, women who seek abortion appear to act against their own best interests. The risk that women are prepared to face can be seen as a measure of the adversity which they expect through continuing an unwanted pregnancy. In societies where the consequence of a pregnancy conceived outside marriage may include withdrawal of family support, social condemnation or death for mother or child, women will choose abortion even when they are aware that the risk is high. Where women enjoy good health and child rearing outside marriage is possible, risks associated with contraception and abortion are less acceptable, both to women and to legislators.

Because contraception is widely used and abortion is very common, it has been possible to collect data concerning the associated risks across diverse populations.[5] Low frequency of complications and low rates of contraceptive failure resulting in a pregnancy have been established. There is strong evidence demonstrating that the risk of death, physical injury, mental injury, or reduction in future fertility are very low following abortions conducted by trained practitioners using appropriate facilities. The risk of death from abortion using surgical[6] or medical[7] procedures is much lower than the risk of childbirth, or other commonly performed surgical procedures, such as caesarean section. Women have lower mortality rates from all causes following an abortion than women who have not been

5. B Winikoff, I Sivin, K Coyaji, *et al*, 'Safety, efficacy, and acceptability of medical abortion in China, Cuba, and India: a comparative trial of mefipristone-misoprostol versus surgical abortion', in *American Journal of Obstetrics and Gynecology*, 176 (1995): 431–37.
6. R Kulier, A Gulmezoglu, G Hofmeyr, L Cheng and A Campana, 'Medical methods for first trimester abortion', in *Cochrane Database of Systematic Reviews*, 4 (2005).
7. R Kulier, A Fekih, G Hofmeyr, and A Campana, 'Surgical methods for first trimester termination of pregnancy', in *Cochrane Database of Systematic Reviews*, 4 (2005).

pregnant.[8] There is no difference in the rates of mental illness amongst women who have had abortions and those who have not.[9] There is no association between abortion and an increased risk of breast cancer.[10] There is some evidence of slightly increased risk of miscarriage or premature labour in subsequent pregnancies following either a miscarriage or an abortion.[11] Both miscarriage and premature labour are relatively common and the increase in risk is small in comparison to the background rate.

There is a significant contrast between the health risk associated with abortions conducted by appropriately trained practitioners using sterile techniques and those conducted in circumstances which do not support safe methods. These differences have been mapped globally by the World Health Organisation[12] in a report which estimates the maternal death rate attributable to unsafe abortion to be 1:270. The harm that restrictive abortion laws cause to women's health and morbidity are well documented and world trends are towards liberalising access to abortion.[13]

Competing interests

Ethical discussion of fertility control may focus entirely on women, overlooking the role of men as reproductive beings with responsibility for their own sexual activity and contraception. Men's rights are most often discussed in relation to a right to paternity rather than in relation to their

---

8. M Gissler, C Berg, M Bouvier-Colle, and P Buekens, 'Pregnancy-associated mortality after birth, spontaneous abortion, or induced abortion in Finland, 1987-2000', in *American Journal of Obstetrics and Gynecology*, 190 (2004): 422–27.
9. A Broen, T Moum, A Bodtker, and O Ekeberg, 'Psychological impact on women of miscarriage versus induced abortion: a two year follow-up study', in *Psychosomatic Medicine*, 66 (2004): 265–71.
10. American College of Obstetrics and Gynecology Committee on Gynecology Practice. AOG Committee Opinion, 'Induced abortion and breast cancer risk', in *International Journal of Gynecology and Obstetrics*, 83 (2003): 233–35.
11. L Henriet and M Kaminski, 'Impact of induced abortions on subsequent pregnancy outcome', in *British Journal of Obstetrics and Gynaecology*, 108 (2001): 1036–42; also Y Sun, Y Che, E Gao, J Olsen, and W Zhou, 'Induced abortion and risk of subsequent miscarriage', in *International Journal of Epidemiology*, 32 (2003): 449–54.
12. World Health Organization, 'Unsafe abortion—global and regional estimates of the incidence of unsafe abortion and associated mortality in 2000', 4th edition, Geneva, 2004; also at www.who.int/reproductive-health/
13. R Cook, B Dickens, and L Bliss, 'International Developments in Abortion Law from 1988 to 1998', in *American Journal of Public Health*, 89 (1999): 579.

own responsibility to constrain their capacity to impregnate and to make ethical decisions about paternity.

Two major areas in which third parties claim rights in relation to abortion are the rights of the foetus and the rights of men to fatherhood.

All claims that a foetus has rights rest on the presumption of the moral personhood of the foetus. If personhood is accorded prior to birth then a claim to the protection of that life follows. The moral status of the foetus is a matter of religious belief for some and for others the stage of development or viability of the foetus (its ability to survive interdependently of its mother) is a marker of personhood. Many jurisdictions accord rights only to born individuals whilst others allow intervention to sustain foetal life against a pregnant woman's wishes, and some outlaw abortion entirely because of the presumption of foetal personhood. Where foetal (or embryonic) personhood is conceded, exercising rights on behalf of the foetus remains incompatible with the principles of the autonomy of, and non-maleficence, towards the pregnant woman.

The ethical principle of proportionality is relevant in weighing competing rights claims, including male rights to paternity. The burden to a woman of continuing a pregnancy unwillingly is generally considered to far outweigh the benefit to the man in becoming a father. Claims by would-be fathers in a pregnancy that they have caused have been given very little legal or ethical standing worldwide. Although cases have been brought in USA and European courts by men seeking to prevent a woman having an abortion these rarely succeed, primarily because recognition of paternal rights contravenes the principles of respect for the woman's autonomy and informed consent. When the principle of proportionality is applied, the rights of the pregnant woman prevail.

Justice

Distributive justice is a key ethical principle which applies to the provision of social goods, including public health services. Health services are an instrumental rather than an absolute good in that they are not good in and of themselves, but only in so far as they facilitate survival, human dignity and full citizenship. The principle of distributive justice requires that health services be accessible to individuals according to need and within the context of resource availability. Where there are barriers preventing access to contraception and abortion, distributive justice is compromised. Access to health care is often stratified by race, class and region. This is also true for access to abortion and contra-ception. Many factors compromise access to fertility control. These include material considerations, cost, availability, and religious or national policies.

Access to safe contraceptive and abortion services requires sufficient regulation of providers and manufacturers to ensure safe services. However, a highly regulated environment can compromise services. In some jurisdictions, regulatory mechanisms retard or restrict the distribution of contraceptives and medications and devices used for post coital contraception and abortion. Currently, this restriction exists in some countries in relation to mefipristone, despite this drug being included on the World Health Organization's list of essential medicines for developing countries.[14]

Access to contraception and abortion are also compromised when services are under attack, and where service providers and or patients are intimidated and stigmatised. The marginalisation of abortion services from mainstream health provision produces further barriers to access. These include difficulties in recruiting, training and sustaining a skilled workforce, which compromise the quality of services.

Stigma associated with abortion and contraception creates an environment where normal requirements for duty of care by medical practitioners can be compromised. For example, where law or practice allows health workers conscientious exemption, those practitioners who decline to provide services still have an ethical obligation to refer the patient for these services elsewhere.

Conclusion

Contraception and abortion are ethical when they result from informed, voluntary decisions by individual women. They support the woman's agency and authority over her own life. They reflect the principle of bodily autonomy and maximise women's opportunities to be healthy. In situations where it is possible to provide contraception and safe abortion, these minimise maternal and infant deaths and enhance the health and social well-being of women and children. It is ethical to provide fertility control services for these reasons.

14. World Health Organization, *Fourteenth WHO Model List of Essential Medicines Disease and Treatment* (Geneva, 2005); also at http://mednet3.who.int/EMLib/

Self-determination and access to contraception and safe abortion are not harmful to women. In contrast, many maternal deaths are caused by unsafe abortion and childbirth without health care. Access to all forms of fertility control, including contraception and safe abortion, are contested across the world, with negative consequences for public health.

Where there are competing claims over a pregnancy, these do not outweigh the ethical value accorded to the autonomy of women and the benefits which flow from self-determination.

The ethical principal of justice supports access to health services for all people. Equitable and confidential access to contraception and abortion are part of any comprehensive public health system.

Contraception and abortion are not the only means of supporting women's self-determination, ability to maximise their health potential or their ability to raise healthy children. Education and economic independence are critical in supporting the well-being of women and their dependents.

Further reading

The Law and Ethics of Abortion: BMA Views (London: British Medical Association, revised 1999).

Royal College of Obstetricians and Gynaecologists, The Care of Women Requesting Induced Abortion (London: RCOG, 2004); also at www.rcog.org.uk

World Health Organization, *Safe Abortion: Technical and Policy Guidelines for Health Systems* (Geneva: WHO, 2003); also at www.who.int/reproductive -health/

Useful Websites

Royal College of Obstetricians and Gynaecologists: www.rcog.org.uk

World Health Organization medicines resources: http://mednet3.who.int/EMLib/

World Health Organization reproductive health resources: www.who.int/reproductive -health/

[This site has a map entitled 'Estimated annual incidence of unsafe abortion per 1000 women aged 15-44 years, by UN subregions 2000'. This is found at p 10 of Unsafe Abortion – global and regional estimates of the incidence of unsafe abortion and associated mortality in 2000, 4th edition.]

Interface Vol 13 1&2/2010

Bioethics and Manipulating the Human Embryo

Greg Pike

Greg Pike
Southern Cross Bioethics Institute
Adelaide, Australia

Introduction

It was once the case that every human life had its origins in the secrecy of the womb. Here was an environment where, if left alone, development and growth could occur and uniqueness unfold. The image is one of protection, nurture and mystery. We are united by this common origin, and with a touch of creative imagination it should not be hard to grasp a sense of the miraculous in the transformative capacity of a single cell to form a whole body. That fingers, eyes, heart and brain all spring from the virtually unseen should still be jaw-dropping. That a single cell possesses the radical capacity for rationality should still draw silence:

> . . . that bud of life that unfurls into existence like a seed that dreams in the snow, in whose secret there stands the tacit awareness of that which lies beyond.[1]

1. Salvino Leone, 'The Ancient Roots of a Recent Debate', in *Identity and Stature of Human Embryo*, Proceedings of the Third Assembly of the Pontifical Academy for Life, February 14-16, edited by Juan De Dios Vial Correa and Elio Sgreccia (Vatican City: Libreria Editrice Vaticana, 1997), 47.

It is sometimes said that technology changes everything and changes nothing. For human embryos,[2] everything changed when fertilisation could first be undertaken outside the body. But nothing changed about the ontological nature of a human embryo. And nothing really changed about the central philosophical questions about human life and its origins and meaning. Perhaps if anything, timeless questions were sharpened by detailed knowledge of human development, but the essential questions remained the same.

Once created outside the human body, embryos were exposed to a new level of vulnerability. Of course, embryos could always be destroyed in abortion as they had been for millennia, but now all sorts of other possibilities have arisen that were never dreamed of in the past. While disease and natural embryo loss have always occurred to a greater or lesser extent, it is in the various forms of manipulation of the human embryo that ethical questions arise. After all, ethics is about what humans ought to do or ought not to do.

When assisted reproductive technology (ART) first occurred in the seventies, and embryos were created *in vitro*,[3] there rapidly followed processes and procedures which either placed embryos at risk of death or involved their direct destruction. Even though embryo research was taking place in the context of ART and its refinement, with the advent of the isolation of human embryonic stem (ES) cells in 1998, research using embryos entered a new phase. Almost eerily juxtaposed in time came the reality

2. The term 'human embryo' means the entity arising from the first contact of sperm and egg up to the end of the eighth week of development. From then on and up to birth the developing human is termed a 'foetus'.
3. Literally meaning 'in glass', *in vitro* fertilisation specifically refers to the creation of an embryo by combining sperm and egg outside the human body in a laboratory setting. The embryo will then continue development in a culture medium in an electronically controlled incubator up until the third to fifth day before being transferred to the woman's uterus, stored for later transfer, used in research or discarded.

of mammalian cloning. Soon, cloned human embryos were produced,[4] followed by human/animal hybrids[5] and even parthenotes[6].

There are two particular drivers behind the desire to manipulate human embryos, whether that occurs in the context of ART or in research. The first is the praiseworthy goal of improving health. Given the suffering caused by numerous human conditions and the proven power of medicine to come up with treatments, there is strong support for the medical/scientific enterprise in general. So it is not surprising that, even amongst those with ethical concerns, support can be found for using embryos in the search for cures.

The second is somewhat deeper, largely unacknowledged and perhaps too under-developed in its modern context to assess properly. It is an enduring strand of endeavour that has been evident in various forms throughout human history: to improve the human species. In the past, that endeavour has taken a more social and cultural path, but now the opportunity for enhancement of the species may take a more technological route.

> The old dreams of the cultural perfection of man [sic] were always sharply constrained by his inherent inherited imperfections and limitations . . . To foster his better traits and to curb his worst by cultural means alone has always been, while clearly not impossible, in many instances most difficult . . . We now glimpse another route—the chance to ease the internal strains and to heal the internal flaws directly, to car-

---

4. UK scientists clone human embryo. See http://news.bbc.co.uk/2/hi /health/4563607.stm
5. Human/animal hybrids have been created in a variety of ways, but most often by introducing a human nucleus into an animal egg. The subsequently formed entity, termed a 'cybrid', has not been allowed to develop beyond a few days, and in any event, is unlikely to be possible. Researchers at Advance Cell Technology in the USA fused a human cell with an enucleated cow's egg to produce an embryo that developed to the 32-cell stage. Stem Cell Sciences in Victoria, Australia, conducted a similar experiment using a pig's egg to produce a 32-cell embryo that was destroyed before further development could take place.
6. In 2001, Advanced Cell Technology in the USA announced production of a parthenogenetically derived human embryo by manipulation of a human egg to develop as an embryo without fertilisation or cloning. See JB Cibelli *et al*, 'The first human cloned embryo', in *Scientific American* 286/1 (January 2002): 44–51, and JB Cibelli *et al*, 'Somatic cell nuclear transfer in humans: pronuclear and early embryonic development', in *Journal of Regenerative Medicine*, 26/2 (November 26, 2001): 25–31.

> ry on and consciously perfect far beyond our present vision this remarkable product of two billion years of evolution.[7]

As the earliest phase of human development, embryos represent the ideal stage at which to enhance. While such specific enhancement is not yet a reality, at the very least the desire for overall improvement has already been expressed in weeding out genetically defective embryos in ART programs. Genetic modifications to embryos to correct disease states will soon follow. After that, or perhaps concurrent with it, will come specific genetic enhancements.

Whether or not human embryos should be manipulated or used for research is part of a much larger question, which relates to the nature of human beings *per se*. It is hard to ignore the fact that within a purely naturalistic account of reality, and therefore of human beings, there is no place for a meta-physical aspect of our nature. Conversely, if humans are more than material, it is hard *not* to likewise acknowledge this aspect in the embryo.

This chapter will discuss some basic embryo science; current manipulations to which human embryos are subject; possible future manipulations yet to be dreamed up by researchers and technicians; how the nature of the human embryo is to be philosophically understood; and finally, what ethical considerations flow from that understanding.

Embryo science

What do we know about human embryos? What has modern science recently unearthed that can assist us in understanding their nature?

The first moment of contact between sperm and egg, typically within the fallopian tube, marks the beginning of the process of fertilisation. This process takes approximately sixteen to twenty-four hours during which the new single-celled entity, termed either zygote or single-celled embryo, is formed. It is a genetically unique individual with the combined, yet as it were pre-mixed,[8] genetic material of both parents. Recent research has revealed that even at this stage, the single-celled embryo has the beginnings

7. Robert Sinsheimer, 'The Prospect of Designed Genetic Change', in *Engineering and Science*, 32 (1969): 8–13.
8. During formation of sperm and eggs, the process known as meiosis involves 'crossing-over' by which genetic mixing occurs. This process increases the genetic diversity of sperm and egg even before conception occurs.

of axis formation and alignment with the point of sperm entry.[9] What is more, after the zygote has divided into two cells at about twenty-four to forty-eight hours, enough specialisation has taken place to cause each cell to pursue different lineages in the developmental process.[10] This finding reveals the rapidity with which 'differentiation' is initiated—the process of specialisation in which the different body cells, tissues and eventually organs are formed.

During the subsequent stages of cellular division, the embryo moves down the fallopian tube to the uterus, where at about five to seven days, the embryo of approximately 200 cells, also termed a blastocyst, implants in the endometrial lining of the uterus and continues development. The blastocyst is like a hollow ball with a collection of cells in the interior, termed embryonic stem (ES) cells, which in the normal course of events develop and differentiate into the body of the embryo. The outer cells form the extra-embryonic tissues like the placenta.

While the early embryo directs its own development, several chemical cues form a line of communication with the mother.[11] Even embryos produced *in vitro*, which are developed in culture media prior to transfer to a woman's uterus, produce 'embryo-derived growth promoting factors'[12] that have a beneficial effect on embryonic development and therefore on the prospect of survival.

At around fourteen days, a structure called the primitive streak begins to appear, which is the very earliest alignment of cells that further differentiate into the nervous system. Up till this stage it is possible for twinning to occur.

The take-home message from early embryology is threefold. First, a new, genetically distinct, individual entity comes into existence at fertilisation, which has the essential genetic and epi-genetic characteristics of

9. K Piotrowska and M Zernicka-Goetz, 'Role for sperm in spatial patterning of the early mouse embryo', in *Nature* 409/6819 (2001): 517.
10. K Piotrowska *et al*, 'Blastomeres arising from the first cleavage division have distinguishable fates in normal mouse development, in *Development*, 128/19 (2001): 3739.
11. CR Austin, *Human Embryos. The Debate on Assisted Reproduction,* (Oxford: Oxford University Press: 1989), 10; also M Mesrogli *et al*, 'Early pregnancy factor as a marker for the earliest stages of pregnancy in infertile women', in *Human Reproduction,* 3/1 (1989): 113.
12. M Almagor *et al*, 'Pregnancy rates after communal growth of preimplantation human embryos in vitro', in *Fertility and Sterility*, 66/3 (1996): 394.

the human species—it is clearly uniquely human and not a kangaroo, fig or newt.

Secondly, early embryonic development is precise and self-directed. The embryo possesses all of the informational content to intrinsically organise itself to develop and mature. The process is active and purposeful. The embryo is no mere clump of cells; it is fundamentally different from any other group of human cells. The visible manifestations of specialisation are evidence of the invisible and mostly unidentified machinations within the cells constituting the embryo. It is likely that we will continue to discover more about the complex, orchestrated and highly directive early stages of embryonic development that are beyond microscopic sight.

Thirdly, the process is a continuum. It is possible to identify markers and key features as development proceeds, but once started and barring misfortune, the process is one of continual development of an entity continuous through time. The special case of twinning will be discussed later.

In summary, the embryo is a whole individual member of the human species at an immature stage of development. Proceeding along its developmental continuum, and on reaching the end of its eighth week, the embryo is now referred to as a foetus. At this point, it has taken on a distinctly human appearance with all of the major organs formed.

Current manipulation

In the seventies, and in the context of ART programs, human embryos became vulnerable in ways they never had been before. The creation of embryos outside of the body for the purpose of transfer to a woman's uterus was, from the very start, experimental. As ART became more widely accepted as a means of providing babies for infertile couples, demand grew for refinement through research. So began experimentation in which embryos were usually, and perhaps inevitably, destroyed in the process. There was and still is research on culture media, freezing and thawing protocols, sperm injection, genetic testing, growth with other types of cells, micromanipulation techniques, embryo splitting, chemical modification, various transfer regimes, and varying implantation conditions. ART research is now a huge field in which embryos in their millions are destroyed for research. As a rapidly growing industry striving for better take-home-baby rates, ART uses human embryos as a laboratory resource. Sometimes it is hard to tell what constitutes research as distinct from quality assurance. Discarding genetically 'unfit' embryos is a form of quality assurance but at the same time information is gained about implantation success or micromanipulation techniques.

Concurrent with ART-based research, other groups began using embryos for different types of research purposes. Basic embryology could now be studied in detail, as could the study of developmental aspects of various disease states. The embryo is also being used to study gene expression and the effects of various chemicals and potential toxins on development. Moreover, fertilisation and implantation is being studied with a view to developing new contraceptives and abortifacient drugs.

In 1998, something happened which was to dramatically increase interest in using human embryos. Researchers at the University of Wisconsin isolated ES cells from an unwanted ART embryo and, by figuring out a way to maintain the cells in culture virtually indefinitely, effectively began the field of human ES cell research.[13] With the ability of ES cells to become any of the 200 or so different types of cells in the human body, the field ran white hot with excitement about the potential applications. There was talk of cures for diseases where a known cell type was defective, like Diabetes and Parkinson's, as well as for complex and poorly understood diseases like Alzheimer's disease, and even predictions of lab-grown organs in the near future. Suddenly, hope was everywhere and embryos were considered essential for this next wave of scientific advance. Although optimism about rapid results has all but evaporated and current thinking is much more circumspect, the impetus for research is as strong as ever.

But there was more to come. The juxtaposition of mammalian cloning[14] in 1997 with the isolation of human ES cells in 1998 raised the possibility that human embryo clones could be created and their ES cells extracted and used for either basic research purposes or for therapies. However, at the time, those arguing most forcefully in favour of the production and use of embryo clones were much more vocal about the possibility that therapies might result from cloning than they were about basic research. Therapeutic cloning,[15] they argued, would eliminate problems of tissue

---

13. JA Thompson *et al*, 'Embryonic stem cell lines derived from human blastocysts', in *Science* 282 (6 November 1998): 1145–47.
14. The cloning of Dolly the sheep in 1997 was soon followed by the cloning of cattle, pigs, mice, rabbits and monkeys.
15. 'Therapeutic cloning' refers to the creation of cloned embryos, followed by the removal of their embryonic stem cells for use in possible therapy. Whilst technically extremely difficult, very expensive, and possibly impractical, therapeutic cloning is appealing because it would theoretically lead to the production of cells, tissues or organs that would not be rejected by the subject of the therapy, the 'clonal parent'.

rejection and lead to the ultimate in tailor-made individual therapies for all of the conditions on the ES cell hope list. At this point in time, while cloned human embryos have been produced, no ES cells from human embryos have successfully been extracted and maintained in culture, let alone put to any use in research or otherwise.

Given the scarcity of human eggs and the large number that would be required to conduct even the most basic human embryo cloning experiment, some scientists have instead produced hybrids by inserting human nuclei into the enucleated eggs of pigs, rabbits or cows. The wisdom of doing so, from either a scientific or ethical perspective, has been strongly challenged. This form of hybrid is really only the tip of the iceberg, and a variety of other forms are possible. Whilst such hybrids are primarily human (at least inasmuch as the human nucleus may be expected to drive development), other types of hybrids could be far closer to fifty/fifty. For example, in what was once a relatively common practice in ART, hamster eggs were mixed with human sperm to test sperm viability. The entity so created was usually allowed to develop up until the first division, further development being highly unlikely in any case. One finds very little discussion about the nature of such an entity.

Despite several claims of cloned human embryos being transferred to women's bodies in the hope of implantation and further development, as far as anyone can reliably tell, this has not happened yet. Not surprisingly, such cloning to birth enjoys very little support.

Future manipulation

In a field such as this, as in so many others in science, there are no guarantees about what may take place next. However, there are certain clues and likely directions.

As more information becomes available about genes and how they function, it is likely that scientists will experiment with genetic modification of the early embryo. In fact, this was recently the subject of considerable debate in the UK's recent amendments to its *Human Fertilisation and Embryology Act*. Permission was granted for genetic modification, but only in a research setting. It is expected that, initially at least, the research will be focused on deleting or correcting defective genes that are known to be associated with disease. However, given that there are already genetic tests available for genes that confer susceptibility to disease and for those that code for non-disease traits, genetic modifications of all sorts will be explored. While initially no such modified embryos will be permitted to be transferred to the body of a woman, the day will eventually come when permission will be granted to transfer an embryo that is genetically modified to be free of certain diseases or of a disease-susceptibility gene. The precedent for this has already been set in ART by using pre-implantation genetic diagnosis (PGD) to select genetically 'superior' embryos for transfer and to discard genetically 'inferior' ones. However, what happens when genetic testing is established to the point that every embryo produced is shown to have some genetic 'defect' or 'limitation' of some kind or another? If an infertile couple is to have a child of their own, then the only option left will be to genetically modify embryos prior to transfer.

Most legislatures that have Acts regulating embryo research choose fourteen days as the limit beyond which embryos are not allowed to develop. Given that this point in time is arbitrary, various arguments notwithstanding, it is difficult to see it standing in the way of a new development with potential therapeutic applications. If a cure for a major disease could be envisioned that required using twenty-eight day embryos, pressure would be applied to extend the limit. Naturally, growing an embryo to this stage *in vitro* would require some advances in another area, namely ectogenesis, which is the artificial womb. So far this field has not produced practical results, but what may be more likely is gestation of a human embryo in the body of an animal. As far back as 1983, ART practitioners conducted rudimentary experiments of this type.[16]

If ES cell research does not produce any results in the field of organ production for transplantation, and knowing that organs are largely complete—at least in form if not size—in the eight week old embryo, it may be appealing to some to use the organs from these embryos or even older foetuses. Of course, organs may already be obtained from aborted foetus-

16. In 1983, IVF pioneer Professor Carl Wood made the following statement: 'At one stage despondency about the technique persuaded the team to try for fertilization of a human egg and sperm cell, and embryo growth, in the sheep. After collecting a mature egg from a patient, we placed it and sperm cells from her husband in the sheep oviduct (the animal equivalent of the fallopian tube). But whereas the sperm cells survived in this environment, we were unable to find any trace of the egg. *In some ways we were relieved at the failure of this experiment as it may have been difficult to convince the community that the sheep was an appropriate place for human fertilization and early human development*' [emphasis added]; Carl Wood and Ann Westmore, *Test-Tube Conception* (Melbourne: Hill of Content Publishing Company, 1983), 48.

es.[17] While size would preclude immediate application, it may be possible for the organs to be grown in the body of a recipient before full functionality is achieved, after which the appropriate connections may be made. Much work would still need to be done, but with the considerable pressure on organ waiting lists, the incentive is high.

A particular limitation to any of the above happening is that embryos belong to someone. That is to say, any embryo produced naturally or in an ART program is the product of sperm from a man and an egg from a woman. It is therefore *their* embryo and they are required to consent to its use for any purpose. However, if sperm and egg could be obtained from another source, detached from immediate human connections, then embryos could be produced with significantly reduced consent issues. As it stands, Australian legislation allows for eggs to be obtained from other sources like aborted foetuses, where consent stands one step further removed from a living person. However, the really significant change will come with the advent of artificial sperm and eggs. This research is closer than one might think.[18] The large-scale production of artificial sperm and eggs would set the embryo research field on a new plane. It would allow for the mass production of embryos one step removed from parents, thereby providing an endless supply of research embryos.[19] It would also mean that, with as many eggs as wanted, cloning could proceed *ad libitum*.

A simple backward glance through the history of ART and embryo research makes all of the above less fanciful than it might initially appear. What is routinely happening now in ART was hardly imaginable a mere twenty-five years ago. The next twenty-five will have many surprises.

---

17. The procurement of tissues from aborted foetuses has occurred most notably in the context of research into treatments for Parkinson's disease. In some cases the technique of abortion was modified to ensure intact delivery so that fresh tissues could be obtained.
18. Michael Le Page, 20 June 2005, 'Further steps towards artificial eggs and sperm'; see http://www.newscientist.com/article/dn7547.
19. Of course, even artificial sperm and egg have the genetic makeup of an individual, so some connection is inevitable. The production of artificial sperm and eggs would also mean that a couple unable to produce their own embryo for the purposes of pregnancy may be able to choose from a variety produced from artificial egg and sperm.

The Nature of the Embryo

It is one thing to know what might be technically achievable, but what ought to be done is something else again: that is a question of ethics. In turn, the answers to curly ethical questions rest upon even more basic philosophical ones. At the core are primary questions about the nature of the human embryo, that is, questions of ontology and metaphysics. While science is good at describing the facts, and technology is able to manipulate facts to certain ends, philosophy is needed to consider the nature of the human embryo and ethics to determine right and wrong action concerning embryos.

In addressing the question 'What is a human embryo?' a good place to start is to ask the question 'What is a human being?' The latter is a prelude to the former because, as we have seen, an embryo is a complete organism of the human species and developmentally continuous with the adult form.

One of the prevalent and problematic conceptions of human beings is based upon dualism. While dualism takes different forms, it can be described as the view that humans are really made of two parts, a mind and body, a soul and body, or a person and body. In each case, the physical substance of the body is conceived of as a separate and, to a certain extent, lesser part. Plato's dualism led him to see the body as an encumbrance, and release from it as an opportunity for the pure soul to be free. Descartes thought the mind was what really mattered and that one could exist without the body. This view of human beings paves the way for seeing embryos or, for that matter, foetuses, the severely mentally disabled, or those at death's door, as material substance without the mind, soul or person. An essentially materialist or physicalist conception of human beings may not seem to suffer from dualist difficulties, but in fact can be seen as a form of dualism in its reduction of what counts about a human being to the physical substrate of the brain and the consciousness arising solely from it. Therefore, humans become essentially valuable because of their conscious physical brain.

Dualism is problematic because it requires the conception of an entity that is part human being or less than fully human in that the material substance can exist without the part that really counts: mind, soul, or person. Dualism is also at odds with the way in which we normally see ourselves on a day-to-day basis; we see ourselves as integrated beings. Our actions arise from conscious decisions in a continuous fashion. We experience a unity in ourselves that makes dualism hard to sustain.

The person/body dualism championed by Singer identifies a minimum set of attributes or characteristics that are considered necessary for the status of personhood and therefore for moral value to apply.

> For Singer, to be a person means being self-conscious, aware of oneself, having plans and projects, desires and interests to be satisfied, being rational, linguistic and interesting—indeed being rather like a University professor.[20]

On this view, the human being gradually comes into being as development proceeds and personhood grows. Indeed, this account of human beings makes it possible for anyone to move in and out of personhood at any stage of development. For at other times in any given human life, disability, disease, frailty or injury may render someone unable to express all the requisite 'personhood' characteristics.

This gradualist idea of human development, the view that sees an entity gradually develop into a full human being at some arbitrary point in time, is an exclusive view of human nature rather than an inclusive one. It is a view that considers the human embryo to be potentially human, but not actually yet a human being. But the notion that humans are only persons when they have certain attributes is not only problematic in application, but logically problematic because it confuses person with personality. It fails to distinguish between what is essential about a human being and what it means to be human, and what are characteristics that human persons have that may or may not be displayed at any one time, or may be expressed to varying degrees. Persons are fundamentally what human beings are, whereas personalities are related sets of human attributes and characteristics. All human lives—at varying stages, as well as from one to another individual—have potentialities. They are not all realised or instantiated at once, but come and go, or may never even be realised at all. For example, persons with disabilities may not be able to express certain functions typically shared by those without disabilities, but their essential nature remains the same. Infants, for example, are a small package of potentialities yet to be realised. They are not the same as adults, but are nevertheless essentially human. Likewise, embryos are essentially human, but even more so a package of potentialities. They do not have the capac-

20. Anthony Fisher and Tracey Rowland, Review of books by Daniel S Oderberg, 'Moral Theory: a Non-Consequentialist Approach', and 'Applied Ethics: a Non-Consequentialist Approach', in *Bioethics Research Notes*, 14/3 (Sept 2002): 25, 26.

ity for the *immediate* expression of certain human functions or abilities, but they certainly have the radical (at root) capacity to do so.

The gradualist view of development into a full human being places considerable emphasis on what are seen as markers of significance during embryonic and foetal development. In fact, the more dedicated gradualist will look for markers of significance even in infants to determine whether personhood is truly present there.[21] The two most common markers chosen in embryological development are implantation at five to seven days and the appearance of the primitive streak at fourteen days. Closely related to the appearance of the primitive streak is the development of consciousness (brain) and the end of possible twinning.

It has been argued that implantation is significant because it marks the beginning of a relationship with the mother, after which time she provides nourishment to the embryo via her blood supply. It is argued that the status of the embryo depends to some extent upon a relationship being formed with the mother. So rather than seeing the embryo as what it is, this line of reasoning emphasises the relationship with the mother as conferring value to the embryo. But this is poor reasoning on at least two counts.

First, as noted above, the early signalling between mother and embryo shows that there is clearly already a relationship in place and that embryo growth and development in the tubal fluids is nourishment. If there were a clear marker of the time at which fertilisation occurs, it is more than likely that a mother would identify this moment as the beginning of her motherhood. Moreover, the textbook definition of pregnancy (being with child) coincides with conception, which in turn is equated with fertilisation. However, the advent of ART has changed things considerably, because in ART, unlike in natural conception, embryos can develop apart from their mothers during the first few days of life. But does this mean that there is no relationship?

Which brings us to the rather obvious second count; relationships of great significance between humans do not always require intimate physical contact. Does not a mother have a relationship with her born child, now separate from her body?

Some consider the appearance of the primitive streak as significant because it represents the first appearance of cells that will give rise to neural

21. For example, see Michael Tooley, *Abortion and Infanticide* (Oxford: Clarendon Press: 1983).

tissue. It also approximately coincides with the time after which twinning does not occur. These two issues will be dealt with separately.

The first appearance of neural tissue—or really its precursors—is said to be significant because it is the very beginning of the formation of the brain and therefore of the development of the roots of consciousness. In fact, the appearance of the primitive streak at about fourteen days has been the basis of legislation in many countries, Australia included, where embryo experimentation is prohibited after this time. As noted in the earlier discussion on dualism, this type of view is reductionist in that it identifies the possible presence of consciousness as the key value, so it shares the same difficulties as brain/body dualism. Furthermore, even if the presence of consciousness really is the key value, then it is more realistic to argue for its development much later, thus making fourteen days appear more arbitrary.[22]

In keeping with this view about the central importance of the brain, some have argued that just as we accept irreversible brain death at the end of life as indicative of the death and non-presence of the person, so we should accept the absence of the brain in the early embryo as indicative of the non-presence of the person. However, this view is fundamentally flawed in that a person at the end of life in whom all brain function has ceased is no longer a self-integrating whole organism. Some functions of the body can be artificially maintained, but the irreversible death of the brain means the end of all possibilities. In contrast, the stage prior to the development of the brain in an embryo marks the beginning of all possibilities. The embryo is a unified organism self-directed towards brain development. It is therefore crucially unlike the brain dead person.

The possibility of monozygotic twinning is also used as an argument to deny that embryos are truly human beings. It is said that because the early embryo possesses the ability to twin it cannot be said to be an individual. And if the embryo is not an individual, a single unified organism, how can it be said to be a human being, because all humans are individuals?

22. In 1999, the author attended the *Therapeutic Cloning for Tissue Repair Forum* in Canberra. One of the speakers was UK Professor Sir Martyn Evans, who was knighted in 2003 and received the Nobel Prize for Medicine in 2007. Professor Evans is regarded by many as the father of embryonic stem cell science. At the forum he said that the decision to choose fourteen days of age had, more than anything else, to do with the fact that this was about the length of time that human embryos could be kept going *in vitro*. His comments reinforce the notion that the choice of the primitive streak and its appearance at approximately fourteen days was arbitrary, and also that a certain expedience dominated the decision.

If the embryo is capable of splitting into two then was it ever truly one?[23] At face value, the idea of two genetically identical entities arising from one does not necessarily rule out the individuality of the original. For example, the sheep from which Dolly was cloned was clearly an individual sheep. Likewise, were human cloning ever to become a reality, we would have no difficulty in recognising the individuality of the clonal parent. But there is another reason why twinning does not deny original individuality. Put simply, if the cells in the early embryo are so independent as to mean that the embryo is just a bunch of cells and not an integrated organism, then why do those cells not *regularly* lead to twinning? Surely what *normally* keeps them together is evidence of the wholeness of an integrated organism? Twinning is a relatively uncommon occurrence,[24] poorly understood, but no reason to deny the biological or conceptual realities about the early embryo.

Before considering various bioethical issues related to human embryos, there is one more matter to consider. With the advent of the creation of different types of embryos, what can we say about their nature? So far, cloned embryos, hybrid embryos, parthenotes and chimeras have been produced, and more unusual ones may follow. What are they? And how like or unlike naturally formed embryos are they? This question is important for several reasons, not the least of which is the claim that cloning humans, now permitted in several legislatures, produces an entity that is different to a sperm and egg embryo—so different as to render cloned embryos devoid of inherent moral value.

A detailed discussion is not possible here. However, one relatively simple observation regarding cloning makes it clear that the cloned embryo is essentially the same as the naturally formed embryo. The observation is that for Dolly, or any other species which has been cloned to birth, the born creature that is developmentally continuous with the cloned embryo is clearly a sheep, mouse, pig, cow or monkey. In other words, Dolly the adult was once Dolly the cloned embryo. Cloned embryos, apart from genetic damage, are the same as naturally formed embryos, otherwise they would not continue developing to their adult form. The fact that cloned human embryos are not transferred to a woman's uterus or that they will

23. This argument has been put rather bluntly as 'There could be one person or two, therefore there's none.'

24. Approximately four per thousand live births.

be so genetically damaged as to have limited chance of survival does not cause them to cease being what they are: cloned human embryos.[25]

Hybrids represent another problem altogether, as do chimeras.[26] If hybrids and chimeras can be produced, detailed biological information will be needed to try to understand their nature. It may be that some forms of hybrid are essentially human,[27] or it may be that there is a clear difference so that another entity altogether has been created. So little is known about parthenotes and whether they represent an embryo with self-integrating organic wholeness that we will have to wait and see.

Bioethics and embryos

Having looked at the nature of the human embryo, it is now necessary to turn to questions of ethics. What is permissible regarding human embryos? What can and cannot be done with them?

Based upon arguments that uphold the status of embryos as full members of the human species, embryos should not be destroyed or otherwise deliberately harmed, even if good may be derived from such actions. Just as more developed members of the species are afforded rights that protect their lives, so embryos should be likewise protected. Such protection should include not placing embryos at significant risk of harm, just as others should not be placed at such risk. The result of following this line of reasoning is that any research involving destruction or harm to embryos should not occur. Furthermore, many of the practices in ART, in which

---

25. There have been several attempts to use different terminology to describe embryos created by unusual means. There has even been an attempt to call sperm and egg embryos by a different name if they are created in an IVF program, are unwanted and handed over for use in research. Louis Guenin coins the term epidosembryos to describe these embryos. The term is taken from the Greek *epidosis*, meaning 'for a beneficence to the common weal'; Louis M Guenin, 'Morals and Primordials', *Science* 292 (1 June 2001): 1659–1660.
26. A chimera is derived from a mix of cells of different genetic origins. The word comes from Greek mythology, where a chimera was a mythical creature part human, and part animal. The word has also come to mean something fanciful or a figment of the imagination.
27. A cybrid is formed by somatic cell nuclear transfer, in which a human nucleus is inserted into an enucleated animal egg. Given that the human genome directs development, it is likely that the entity so formed will be essentially human. However, so little is known about epigenetics and cytoplasmic influence upon development, that the nature of such a hybrid will remain uncertain.

embryos are deliberately destroyed or discarded or placed in a position of exposure to high risk of harm, should not occur.

Ethical arguments which do permit such harm are, typically, based upon consequentialism, in which embryos may or may not be afforded a high moral status, even though low or insignificant moral status is more typical. If embryos have low or no moral status it is really a no brainer regarding what might be permissible. Pretty much anything goes. But even if embryos are accorded a high moral status, arguments can be mounted on consequentialist grounds that permit their destruction. One of these will be discussed shortly, but first there is an observation that is often used to argue that embryos should be afforded a low moral status.

This observation concerns the fact that a significant number of early human embryos formed naturally by the union of sperm and egg never implant and therefore perish, or otherwise perish soon after. Various figures have been quoted even though evidence specific to natural human reproduction is scant. Natural embryo loss is variously placed in the range of twenty to eighty per cent. The detection of urinary human chorionic gonadotrophin (HCG) as a measure of 'chemical pregnancy' was carried out by Miller and co-workers[28] and taken as a post-implantation measure from which the authors deduced that 42.8% of embryos were lost, and 57.2% resulted in live births.

It is argued by some that natural embryo loss shows that embryos could not possibly be human beings, because no Creator would permit such catastrophic loss of innocent human life. The argument is also thought to be bolstered by the observation that no-one really grieves appropriately for such loss, nor attempts to do anything about it. In either case, those who use this argument are basically saying that because nature causes the demise of embryos, so can we. What nature does, we can likewise do.

There are several responses. First, much of what is called embryo loss may not even be that. In fact, it may be that fertilisation does not even proceed in a fashion consistent with the formation of an embryo. Instead, many of the resulting entities may be products of such serious errors of formation that they are not embryos at all. That is, they are not whole self-integrating organisms. Secondly, natural embryo loss is just that—natural. It is not, as far as we can tell, a result of human action. Therefore, any argument that aims to justify destroying human embryos because nature does so, fails as a naturalistic fallacy. Hume ruthlessly exposed this error

28. JF Miller *et al*, 'Fetal loss after implantation—a prospective study', in *Lancet* 13/2; 8194 (Sept 3, 1980): 554–56.

which sought to justify *immoral* actions based upon *amoral* ones. After all, at various times in human history, natural infant loss has been as high as fifty per cent, but that tells us nothing about the moral value of infants. In essence, this problem is really about the problem of evil, and why a just and good God could permit such things. Thirdly, with regard to grieving and doing something about such loss, this view fails to recognise that we likewise do not grieve over the massive worldwide natural loss of life due to say malnutrition nor do enough about it. But more importantly, there are various practical limitations we and our communities have regarding a loss that is so diverse, poorly understood and largely undetectable.

It is now necessary to turn to an argument that has proven popular in public debate. This argument starts with the fact that millions of human embryos are stored in deep freeze in ART programs around the world. Many of these embryos will be unwanted and therefore allowed to succumb, that is, be removed from liquid nitrogen and allowed to die. This is often mandated by legislation. The argument goes that since these embryos are going to die anyway, they may as well be used in research and not be wasted. But if those arguing this way do in fact place a high moral value upon embryos, it is not an argument they would make for other human lives. None would presumably support organ removal from those soon to die, thereby causing their death, on the grounds that they are going to die anyway. Would they? As it turns out, many if not most of those running this line of argument do not actually consider human embryos worthy of protection, making the 'going-to-die-anyway' argument appear disingenuous.

The moral difficulties that are inherent in the *ex vivo* production of human embryos and their freezing cannot somehow be balanced up by taking the further step of intentionally killing embryos for scientific or medical gain. While there may be some collective bad conscience for allowing embryonic human beings to exist in suspended animation, it will not be salved by using them as research material. We have made for ourselves a 'Sophie's Choice'. The crucial element is that human choice has determined that there will be frozen embryonic human beings. It has been human action that has produced millions of frozen human lives, even though perhaps at the time with 'eyes wide shut' to the consequences. We decide that they should die, then we say that they are going to die anyway, so we may as well gain some benefit. This form of argument is disingenuous.

A more straightforward utilitarian argument can be mounted that proposes the destruction of embryos purely on the grounds that good can be achieved. This is the same type of moral reasoning that would permit the sacrifice of some lives in other contexts so that the 'greater good' can be served. In other words if, on balance, more good can be achieved than wrong done by destroying embryos, then the destruction can be justified. Besides the immediate moral problem that utilitarian reasoning like this can be used to justify the direct killing of innocent human beings, the putative good to be achieved is so speculative that any balancing is seriously out of kilter. In any case, utilitarian calculations like this are an attempt to measure the immeasurable. What scales does one use to weigh innocent human lives or speculative health outcomes?

The proposal to use cloned human embryos to obtain stem cells for possible tailor-made treatments or for investigations into disease-specific stem cell lines carries with it an additional risk. There are already bioethicists of considerable standing who have argued for cloning to birth in certain circumstances.[29] Given the ethical slide that is now commonplace in ART, proposals of this sort are not really all that surprising. The fact that several legislatures have permitted the cloning of human embryos means that much of the primary technical groundwork will be laid for the subsequent almost irresistible urge some scientists will have to transfer cloned embryos to women's bodies. Couple this with the justifications provided by some key, albeit out-on-a-limb bioethicists, and attempts at cloning to birth may become commonplace.

One remaining ethical issue of very real significance is that good alternatives to using human embryos exist. Space precludes an adequate discussion except to say that a case can easily be made that the alternatives are already yielding better results and may continue to do so. For example, research and clinical trials using various adult stem cells instead of embryonic ones are well advanced and in some cases in therapeutic application for a diverse range of conditions. In a pluralistic society in which different ethical perspectives exist, there is an imperative to first pursue research that does not evoke strong opposition, before any consideration of that which does.

29. M Warnock, *Making Babies: Is There a Right to Have Children?* (Oxford: Oxford University Press, 2002).

Conclusions

The public debate of recent years about whether or not human embryos should be used for research or in therapeutic treatments is part of a much wider debate that has to do with differing worldviews. The same elements can be found in the abortion and euthanasia debates, and even in discussions about disability, genetics and reproductive technologies. Sometimes the ferocity with which those debates have raged is a clue to what may be at stake. One can use all the reasonable philosophical and technical argument in the world, but sometimes it can appear as if people end up just talking past one another. The debates are important, for they are not just abstract discussions about philosophy and belief but about the types of societies we wish to build and the things that truly enable human beings to flourish and lead whole and abundant lives.

At the core are different conceptions of human life itself and of our place in the natural order. The basic belief that humans have a particular inherent dignity or sanctity gives essential meaning and a unique status to human life. It is the type of view that recognises something commonly shared by all humanity at every stage of development and without distinction. What adults, children and infants have that makes them valued is the very same something which makes foetuses and embryos likewise valued.

In this chapter it has been argued that human embryos from the moment of conception are human beings. As the youngest members of the human family they ought to share the same protections that other humans enjoy. It follows that procedures and practices which involve either harming or destroying embryos in research or treatment, or otherwise placing them at risk of harm, are unjust and unethical.

Life as Loss?

Bernadette Richards

Bernadette Richards
University of Adelaide
Adelaide, Australia

Can life ever be considered a loss? Is there any point at which the law is prepared to define existence as something worthy of compensation? Or, perhaps even more startling, is there a point at which the law is prepared to favourably compare non-existence with existence? Will the law pause at either of the borders of life and cast its jurisprudential eye over the other side of the border and say, Yes, it would be better if this individual had never crossed the initial border into life, or it would be better if this individual crossed over the other border into death?

On the face of it, the answer to each of these questions is a clear No. One of the driving principles of the law is the sanctity of life, a foundational principle that is universal in its appeal. However, there are situations in which individuals have come before the courts arguing that either their life or (perhaps more disquieting to some) their child's life ought to be defined as a legally cognisable loss. Such an alarming claim has resulted in some judicial acrobatics revealing an underlying aversion to the concept that life, on any level, can be defined as a loss. In doing this the law has turned its face from plaintiffs who have not only suffered a significant wrong at the hands of another but will also bear the ongoing consequences of this wrong for many years.

It is my aim in this discussion to demonstrate that in these situations there clearly is a loss which ought to be recognised by the law but it is not, in truth, a question of whether or not life itself is a loss. The plaintiffs in each case have not set out to define living as a loss but they have argued that, because of the actions of another party their life is not as it ought to be. There has been a clear detriment suffered as a result of the careless actions of another. In asking whether life is a loss the courts have misdirected the enquiry and failed to address adequately the true issue before them.

The law

The law is a discipline of language and labels and the two relevant labels here are 'wrongful life' and 'wrongful birth.' An action for wrongful life is brought by a child for failing to prevent them from being born, while the wrongful birth claims are brought by the parents of an unintended child. Much is revealed about the accepted approach to these two complaints when one considers the labels: the focus is clearly on the supposed wrongfulness of either the birth or life. The law is thus called upon to address the question of whether the life or the birth is wrong and, instinctively, the response to this is negative. If, however, the focus were on the wrong (rather than on the question of life) then perhaps the response would be quite different. This position will become clearer once two illustrative examples are considered.

Before explaining the examples I will, however, pause and, with the non-legal reader in mind, provide a brief overview of the legal framework within which these decisions were made. The relevant area of law is negligence and in order to succeed in a negligence claim the aggrieved person (the plaintiff) must demonstrate that the defendant owed them a duty to meet an established standard of care. For example, the driver of a car owes a duty of care to all of their passengers to drive as a careful, prudent driver. If the defendant has failed to meet that standard of care (has driven recklessly), then it is said that they have breached their duty of care. The plaintiff must then establish that the breach of duty caused the loss or injury they sustained; for example, the reckless driver drove off the road and into a tree causing the plaintiff to sustain a physical injury. The court will then determine the appropriate damages to be awarded and these damages are aimed at placing the plaintiff in the position they would have been in if the defendant had not acted in a negligent manner. Thus, at its most basic, the law requires the court to determine whether the defendant acted in a manner that was inconsistent with expectations and, in so acting, caused some loss or injury to the plaintiff.

Turning first to wrongful birth, the High Court of Australia in *Cattanach v Melchior* (2003) 215 CLR 1 (*Cattanach*), determined that parents can indeed recover damages for the birth of a child conceived following a (failed) sterilisation procedure.[1] The Melchiors had two healthy children when they decided, on financial grounds, that their family was complete. During consultations with Dr Cattanach, Mrs Melchior informed him that it was her understanding that her right ovary and fallopian tube had been removed during an appendectomy when she was fifteen years old. In reality, only her right ovary had been removed, leaving her right fallopian tube intact (it was, however, obscured from sight by scar tissue and therefore not readily apparent to Dr Cattanach during the operation). Jordan Melchior was conceived by transmigration of an ovum from the left ovary to the right fallopian tube, and born in 1997. It was found that Dr Cattanach had performed the operation with all due care and skill but was negligent in the advice provided prior to the operation (the negligence lay in the failure to warn of the increased risk of pregnancy if her information were incorrect). The question before the court was whether or not the birth of Jordan (and thus the financial burden of his upbringing) was a legally cognisable loss.

The case proceeded through the Supreme Court and the Court of Appeal in Queensland to the highest court of appeal in this country: the High Court of Australia. There were five main arguments used to challenge the Melchiors' claim, each of which were clearly set out in the joint judgment of Justices McHugh and Gummow:[2]

1. Immunity: There ought to be a level of immunity granted to the healthcare profession for failed sterilisation procedures.
2. Public policy: The awarding of damages for the birth of a healthy child is against public policy.
3. Blessing: A child is a blessing and a benefit for parents and thus, there is no compensable harm.
4. Psychological damage: The potential for the infliction of psychological harm on the 'unwanted child' if such ac-

1. The facts as outlined are taken from the judgment in general and, more specifically, from the judgment of Callinan J at [273]ff.
2. *Cattanach v Melchior* (2003) 215 CLR 1, [41] – [92].

tions are sanctioned by the courts is so great that such actions should be refused.

5. Set off: This argument is related to the blessing argument but differs in that the benefit of the healthy child is to be set off against any award of damages, thus reducing, or completely negating, those damages.

Once each of these arguments is scrutinised it becomes clear that the driving force behind them is a concern that life itself will be challenged or cheapened. The economic reality of parents who had decided, in the interests of their existing family unit, not to extend their limited financial resources further by having more children is completely overlooked. The misdirection of the enquiry is clear and the realities of the Melchiors' situation is pushed aside in the interests of protecting the driving principle of sanctity of life.

In this instance the majority of the High Court was able to look beyond the diverting arguments and determine that yes, there was a loss here. Most importantly, Justices McHugh and Gummow acknowledged, indeed emphasised, that the law is concerned with the value of life and the welfare of children,[3] but emphatically rejected this as grounds for denying the claim. Their Honours noted that, in situations such as this, it is not correct to focus on either the parent-child relationship or the child himself as the harm; rather, it is the burden of the legal and moral responsibilities that ought to be the focus.[4] The realities of the life as a loss debate and aversion to treating children as a commodity were also acknowledged by Justice Callinan who openly admitted that he found the process of assessing damages in this instance 'personally distasteful',[5] but referred to legal principle and was able to put aside his aversion and undertake the process required by law.

Three of the High Court judges[6] were, however, unable to look away from the reality of a healthy child being considered in purely financial terms and felt unable to separate the economic question from the moral one. Chief Justice Gleeson emphasised the 'fundamental value' that the common law places on human life,[7] and declined to compartmentalise

3. *Cattanach v Melchior* (2003) 215 CLR 1, [56].
4. *Ibid*, [67]–[68].
5. *Ibid*, [296].
6. Chief Justice Gleeson, Justice Hayne and Justice Heydon.
7. *Ibid*, [6].

the parent/child relationship into discrete financial and moral considerations. It was essential, in his view, that this relationship be viewed holistically, as a relationship with multiple aspects and consequences, 'some of which are economic, some which are not; some of which are beneficial and others which are detrimental.'[8] Most significant, in his Honour's view, was the fact that a child is not a commodity 'that can be sold or otherwise disposed of',[9] and the essence of life and family relationships here amounted to an insurmountable obstacle to the parents' claim. Similarly, Justice Heydon emphasised the inherent and unique value of human life which renders the birth of a child incapable of estimation in monetary terms.[10] The position of the three judges who disagreed with the majority here is best summed up by his Honour's description of the whole process of parents coming to court seeking recompense for the birth of their child as an 'odious spectacle.'[11]

How then did the community respond? As can be imagined, the decision of the High Court to award damages in these circumstances was not well received. In the view of the public, the Court had found that a child (and therefore a life) amounts to an economic loss and the decision was deemed to have challenged fundamental family and societal values. This is a view reflected in the response of the Hon John Anderson (acting Prime Minister at that time) in a press release in which he stated that he was 'deeply concerned' by the decision and described the conclusion of the High Court that the birth of a healthy child can be the subject of damage as 'repugnant.' Mr Anderson went on to ask whether we 'have so lost sight of the sanctity of life and the enormous joy and privilege of nurturing children emotionally and physically that we cannot see the importance of treating them as more than mere commodities?'[12] This response was a common one, which prompted swift reaction from three States with legislation now prohibiting the award of damages in situations such as this.[13]

---

8. *Ibid*, [27].
9. *Ibid*, [35].
10. *Ibid*, [347].
11. *Ibid*.
12. Media Response to *Cattanach v Melchior*, Press release 17 July 2003, A80/2003, Hon John Anderson, MP, acting Prime minister.
13. *Civil Liability Act 2002* (NSW), s 71 (limitation of the award of damages for the birth of a child) which prohibits the award of damages for costs associated with the rearing or maintaining of the child, including loss of earning capacity; and *Civil Liability Act 2003* (Qld), ss 49A and 49B (as per the New South Wales legislation this includes a prohibition on recovery of damages for child rearing costs and covers failed

Thus, despite the Melchiors stating clearly that they loved Jordan and that they did not wish to devalue him as a human being, the focus moved beyond the individual family seeking a solution to a financial detriment suffered, in their view, as the result of the negligence of a trusted healthcare professional. The decision came to stand for something more, for (in the words of Mr Anderson) 'an undermining of the family unit and a cheapening of all life which constituted a threat to our cherished freedom.'[14]

What then of the child who challenges her own existence? This was the issue confronting the High Court in *Harriton v Stephens* (2006) 226 CLR 52 (*Harriton*). The underlying complexities of this action are reflected in the diversity of the judgments. Whilst there were clear endeavours to appeal to legal principle and to place the (to many) disturbing question of whether non-existence would be preferable to existence with disabilities within an accepted legal framework, the High Court judges found it difficult to overcome that one key question. The attempts to place the decision within the framework of legal principle were undermined by the repeated reversion to value-laden language, reflecting the majority judicial view that challenges such as this should not succeed.

Alexia Harriton was born profoundly disabled as a result of exposure to rubella whilst in utero.[15] Her mother had experienced a fever and rash and, suspecting that she was pregnant, consulted Dr Stephens (senior, now deceased) expressing concern that the fever was rubella and that she was pregnant. She had blood tests which indicated that she was indeed pregnant and had been exposed to rubella. Mrs Harriton then consulted Dr Stephens (junior, the defendant in the case) who informed her that she was pregnant but assured her that the rash was not rubella. The action was brought on the basis of this latter assurance and it was accepted by all parties that, if she had been given the correct advice, the pregnancy would have been terminated and Alexia would never have been born. The action here was brought by Alexia as her mother was out of time,[16] and the basis of her claim was that Dr Stephens had been negligent in failing to

---

sterilisation procedures as well as failed contraceptive procedure or contraceptive advice); similarly *Civil Liability Act 1936* (SA), s 67 (specifically excludes recovery for the ordinary costs of bringing up a child, conceived as a result of failed sterilisation procedures, contraceptive procedures etc).

14. Media Response, above note 12.
15. The facts are drawn from the published judgment.
16. All negligence actions have specific time limitations, set by the relevant *Limitation of Actions Act* in each State or Territory. For personal injury, this is usually three years. It is important to note that Alexia herself lacked legal capacity, so the action

inform her mother of the exposure to rubella, thus denying her the opportunity to terminate the pregnancy. This claim gave rise to clear conceptual problems, which saw the Court struggling to see beyond the foundational sanctity of life principle.

One of the main aims of negligence law is to place the plaintiff in the position they would have been in if there had been no negligence. Such a process clearly involves a comparison of what would have been and what is.[17] This comparator approach presented an insurmountable obstacle for the majority of the Court and Alexia was unsuccessful in her action.

Justice Hayne sought to frame his decision in legal principle, yet revealed an underlying value judgment in his conclusion that the common law *should* not be developed in the way contended by Alexia Harriton. In his view, the defining concept in negligence law is the existence of damage and here, where there is life (when the alternative is non-existence) there can be no legally recognised damage. Significantly, the appellant (Alexia), had specifically disavowed the argument that the appropriate comparison was with an 'able bodied' person; rather, it was with never having been born, as that is what would have been the case if the doctor had not been negligent.[18] It was upon this apparent impossibility of comparison that Justice Hayne hung his conclusion that there was no legally relevant damage here.

The impossibility of the comparator was the cornerstone of Justice Crennan's judgment.[19] In her Honour's view, it was not that the comparison between existence and non-existence was difficult or problematic; it was that it was impossible and would amount to the creation of a fiction.[20] While there are possible problems with the comparator approach, these are not insurmountable (and will be discussed further below), and it is important to pause and consider the language employed by her Honour. Of great concern to Justice Crennan was the value of life and the fact that, in the eyes of the common law of Australia, all human beings are valuable and the complexity of the human condition is respected.[21] In her view, it was 'odious' and 'repugnant' to devalue the life of a disabled person by

---

was brought on her behalf. Thus any reference to Alexia's claim is really to the claims made by her representative.

17. *Harriton v Stephens* (2006) 226 CLR 53, per Justice Hayne [168].
18. Ibid, [170].
19. Both Chief Justice Gleeson and Justice Gummow concurred with Justice Crennan and therefore, did not present an individual judgment.
20. *Harriton v Stephens* (2006) 226 CLR 53. [265]–[266].
21. *Ibid*, [258].

suggesting that they would be better off not having being born.[22] Once again, therefore, we see a judge who is focussing on the broader question of the sanctity of life and perhaps overlooking the nuances of the claim before the court. Yet, there is a level of unease with the clear statement of reasons encompassing intangibles such as value of life evidenced by her retreat into apparent legal principle with claims that the law will not provide relief where a comparison is impossible.

Justice Callinan did not, however, retreat from the true nature of his concerns and openly acknowledged the role of value judgments and the complexities of the issue, explaining that what was before the court was more than a mere legal question.[23] His honour pointed out that the question rested on ethical foundations,[24] which have exercised the minds of philosophers, theologians, scientists, legislators and lawyers throughout the world,[25] without there being any well defined response. Despite the ethical complexities and ongoing discussions about legal policy, his Honour found a simpler response. In his view, the whole discussion was based upon an illogical precept: 'It is not logically possible for any person to be heard to say "I should not be here at all", because a non-being can say nothing at all.' [26] It was on this ground that he rejected Alexia's claim.

Many of the issues raised by the majority of the judgments were, however, adequately addressed by the dissenting judgment of Justice Kirby and it is the themes touched upon by his Honour that will form the basis of the rest of our discussion. In his judgment, Justice Kirby sought to redirect the enquiry away from emotive and—to some extent—irrelevant concerns towards the realities of Alexia Harriton's situation. He emphatically rejected the value-laden label and suggested the alternative of 'wrongful suffering',[27] thus shifting the focus away from the insurmountable problems associated with challenging the worth of life. In his endeavour to redirect the enquiry, Justice Kirby emphasised that Alexia did not claim that her life was wrongful, nor did she contend that it now ought to be terminated. Rather, the wrong was her ongoing and unrelieved suffering which could have been averted if the defendant (Dr Stephens) had not been negligent. According to Justice Kirby the answer here lay in a

22. *Ibid*, [259].
23. *Ibid*, [184].
24. *Ibid*, [199].
25. *Ibid*, [184].
26. *Ibid*, [205].
27. *Ibid*, [6].

'decoding' of the issues by reference to legal analysis, [28] and, in direct contrast to Justice Callinan, he argued that if one were to apply logic alone, it would mean that the wisdom of the law in responding to novel problems would be defied.[29] He challenged the view that relief must be denied because of the implausibility of the comparator (between existence and non-existence) on the basis—correct in my view—that this is little more than a convenient sidestepping of the true issue and a convenient denial of the willingness of the law in other situations to compare the tangible with the intangible.[30] Of most significance in this judgment is his approval of comments from a United States decision that we need not retreat into the mysteries of life to answer the legal question, as the reality is that the plaintiff both exists and suffers because of the actions of another.[31]

The words of Justice Kirby bring us back to the question of labels and the issue of whether the focus ought to be on a life or a birth that is wrong, or whether it is better to focus on the actual wrong? It is this misdirection of the enquiry which is of concern and has resulted in a misapplication of legal principles in order to protect a perceived threat to the sanctity of life principle.

Why the misdirection?

Before placing the enquiry back on track, it is important to identify why there has been a misdirection in the first place. Why is it so hard for the judges to step back from the complexities of the ethical, theological and philosophical question of the value of life? What is it about the framing of the claims that prevents the law (and society) from lifting their eyes from the diverting questions to the true issue of whether one party has acted in a manner detrimental to another? In reality, the greatest hurdle before any claimant in a wrongful life/birth case is the predominant view of the courts that, in allowing such an action, they openly challenge the sanctity of life and undermine some foundational societal principles, including family values, moral worth and the inherent (as opposed to economic) value of a human life.

---

28. *Ibid*, [14].
29. *Ibid*, [87].
30. *Ibid*, [101]. Refer also to the discussion below on the House of Lords decision in *Airedale NHS Trust v Bland* [1993] AC 789.
31. *Ibid*, [60], citing with approval Jefferson PJ (with whom Lillie and Rimerman JJ agreed) in *Curlender v Bio-Science Laboratories*, 165 Cal Rptr 477 at 488 (1980).

It is perhaps a simple case of deliberate misdirection by defendants. It is, of course, in the defendant's interest for such claims to fail. Why not then raise issues of commodification of children and sanctity of life? As Lee points out, these arguments raised in defence of wrongful life/birth claims are of 'dubious philosophical pedigree, inconsistent with other legal standpoints and (serve to) obscure the issue.'[32] It really amounts to a legal sleight of hand: direct the attention towards the 'abhorrent'[33] job of placing an economic value on life and the true issue of responsibility for a harm suffered at the hands of another is put to one side. How then can the law be directed back to the true issue? Is it possible to overcome the 'legal quagmire'[34] created by the appeals to underlying ethical and moral debates and actually apply legal principles to an otherwise straightforward question: Did one party act in such a way as to make the life of another difficult? Was this action inconsistent with the duty of care owed to that person? If the answer to these questions is Yes, then a clear application of negligence principles means that there ought to be recompense.

Justice Kirby in *Harriton* clearly felt that such an approach would be possible, as did the majority of the High Court in *Cattanach*. The question remains therefore: *how* can the legal enquiry be put back on track and how can the question of whether or not life itself amounts to a loss be put to one side?

Addressing the diversions (getting back on track)

Each of the diversions placed in the path of the judiciary can be rationally (and ethically) addressed. The enquiry in these cases begins to go astray right from the start with the emotive mislabelling of 'wrongful birth' and 'wrongful life.' As Justice Kirby pointed out in *Harriton*, such labelling is 'value-laden', 'uninstructive, misleading' and, above all, 'decidedly unhelpful'.[35] His Honour went on to emphasise that the 'alleged wrong is not in any meaningful sense the cause of the plaintiff's existence . . . and [as an] epithet it misdescribes the essential nature of the complaint.'[36]

32. Robert Lee, 'To Be or Not to Be: Is that the Question? The Claim of Wrongful Life', in R Lee and D Morgan, *Birthrights: Law and Ethics at the Beginnings of Life* (Routledge, 1989), 188–90.
33. Carel JJM Stolker, 'Wrongful Life: The Limits of Liability and Beyond,' in *International and Comparative Law Quarterly*, 43 (1994): 521, 526.
34. Lee, above note 32, 174.
35. *Harriton v Stephens* (2006) 226 CLR 53, [6] and [8].
36. *Ibid*, [9] – [10].

Others have described the labelling as 'an emotive misclassification',[37] 'unfortunate', and erecting a 'symbolic barrier to recovery [due to] bizarre, even macabre overtones.'[38]

But what is the true issue with the label? How does it so significantly divert, and thus derail, the complainant's case? The problem can be found in the linking of 'wrongful' with 'birth' or 'life' as it focuses the enquiry on the essence of humanity and sanctity of life. The linking of the notation of a wrong with either life or birth causes the judges (and therefore the law) to retreat in some haste from the enquiry, largely on the basis of an aversion to mounting any challenge to the core principle of sanctity of life. We see judges simply 'refusing to conduct the investigation because of ethical or religious beliefs'[39] and constructing apparently sound principled and policy based obstacles to success in these claims. Such obstacles include the impossibility of a comparator (that is, existence and non-existence cannot and will not be compared at law), the absence of harm (based upon life as a blessing and the natural process of reproduction) and the catch-all concern of public policy prohibiting such an enquiry. As will be demonstrated in the discussion below, each of these obstacles can be deconstructed and the true essence of the claim addressed through a careful application of uncontroversial legal principle.

No loss here (blessing and offset):

The essence of this argument is that, while there may have been a wrong (a medical practitioner failed to provide the appropriate standard of treatment), there is no identifiable loss.[40] This conclusion is reached by two routes. The first is, quite simply, that there is life and where there is life there is benefit and these circumstances simply cannot fall within the legal definition of damage.[41] The second route lies in the blessing and offset argument. This springs from the view that all life amounts to a blessing

37. Lee, above n.32.
38. Harvey Teff, 'The Action for "Wrongful Life" in England and the United States', in *International and Comparative Law Quarterly*, 34 (1985): 423, 425.
39. Allan Beever, *Rediscovering the Law of Negligence* (Oxford: Hart Publishing, 2007), 386.
40. It is important to note that this discussion centres around the circumstances when the treatment was negligent, and does not apply where the sterilisation procedure spontaneously fails.
41. G Tedeschi, 'On Tort Liability for "Wrongful Life"', in *Israel Law Review*, 1 (1966): 513, 530.

and thus a child, whether initially wanted or not, will always amount to a blessing. In addition to this, there are also proponents of the 'offset' argument which holds that, while there may be a financial cost to the rearing of a child, this can be offset by the overwhelming benefits to be gained from the joy of parenthood.

If we begin with the offset argument,[42] it soon becomes apparent that it is entirely inconsistent with the general approach of the law in other areas. This reality was discussed by Lord Clyde in the English decision of *McFarlane v Tayside Health Board* where he noted that it was inconsistent with principle to attempt to set off factors of quite a different character against each other.[43] The issue here is with the joy and love of parenting being used to reduce the economic realities of feeding, clothing and educating (to name a few) a child. There is no other context in a negligence claim where the law engages in a cost/benefit calculation,[44] and to do so here undermines the financial realities. If, for example, my slightly dilapidated house is destroyed in a fire caused by the negligence of a neighbour, the court, in awarding damages for the building of a new house and replacement of my furniture, cups, plates and so on, does not engage in a balancing equation whereby the expense incurred is not met because I have the 'blessing' of a sparkling new kitchen and crockery minus the chips. These two issues are, quite rightly, viewed as totally separate.

To acknowledge the expense of raising a child is not to devalue that child; it is merely to acknowledge the day-to-day reality. This is particularly so in families in the position of the Melchiors who were on a restricted income and made a carefully thought out decision to limit the size of their family. They did not do this because they devalued their existing children or because they thought children were little more than a detriment. On the contrary, they decided to exercise their reproductive autonomy and limit the size of their family on purely financial grounds: they simply could not afford any more children.

The reality is that society accepts that children will not always amount to a blessing. This acceptance is implicit in the availability of the sterilisation procedures which are ethically, medically and legally sanctioned. Families such as the Melchiors have made a well founded decision and sought the appropriate medical treatment. This treatment was provided

42. This argument is usually limited to the context of the 'wrongful birth' claims and this portion of the discussion will also be limited to these particular claims.
43. *McFarlane v Tayside Health Board* [2000] 2 AC 59, 103.
44. Emily Jackson, *Medical Law: Text, Cases and Materials* (Oxford: OUP, 2006), 668.

negligently and failed. Emily Jackson makes a good point when she asks how the failure of a medical procedure, specifically undertaken to avoid the 'benefits' of parenthood, can possibly be described as a blessing?[45] What we have here is a damage of a different kind. It has been described as an injury of a 'socially constructed kind'[46] amounting to a loss of control over an individual's (or in a broader sense, a whole family's) 'moral, relational and social lives'.[47] The focus of the law here should be on the economic detriment suffered by a family when they have decided that it is in their best interests to control the size of the family. It should not be on the legally irrelevant issue of whether or not the child is a blessing so as to override the detriment which is of a completely different type. It cannot be concluded that everything about having a child is an unremitting blessing that overrides all financial realities. Indeed, as Allan Beever points out, 'If all children were a blessing then family planning would be irrational.'[48]

No possible comparator and a refusal to devalue the disabled:

The overriding concern with respect to the wrongful life claim is the apparent impossibility of the comparison between life and death. As pointed out in *Harriton* the issue of non-existence and what there is beyond the boundaries of life has exercised the minds of philosophers, theologians, scientists, legislators and lawyers[49] the world over. Such a question has been deemed to be beyond the realm of the courts, and the practical impossibility of engaging in this comparison in a meaningful way has been cited as the foundational reason for rejecting these claims. The mere thought of attempting to 'devalue' the life of one person by intimating that they would have been better off if they had never been born has provided the impetus for judges to retreat behind (apparent) legal principle and reject these claims outright. It has also enabled the use of strong, apparently ethically grounded, language expressing judicial distaste at even being invited to participate in such a distasteful comparison.[50] Whilst it may appear that the judges have adopted the high moral ground, which they

45. *Ibid*, 669.
46. Christian Witting, 'Physical Damage in Negligence', in *Cambridge Law Journal*, 61/1 (2002): 189, 194.
47. Nicolette Priaulx, *The Harm Paradox: Tort Law and the Unwanted Child in an Era of Choice* (Oxfordshire: Routledge-Cavendish, 2007), 48.
48. Beever, above note 39, 392.
49. *Harriton v Stephens* (2006) 226 CLR 53, [184].
50. Refer to the discussion of the decision in *Harriton* outlined above.

claim is consistent across all areas of the law, such a claim does not bear close scrutiny as the law has, in other contexts, happily engaged in the calculation of damages where the immediate loss is difficult to identify. It has also quite comfortably acknowledged that there are circumstances in which life is not, perhaps, the most favourable alternative.

An illustrative case here comes from the House of Lords, *Airedale NHS Trust v Bland* (*Bland*).[51] In this instance, seventeen-year-old Anthony Bland was injured in the Hillsborough soccer riots and suffered from 'catastrophic and irreversible damage to the higher centres of the brain . . . leaving him in a persistent vegetative state.'[52] The parents brought the issue before the court, seeking permission for the removal of Anthony's feeding tube (with the outcome being his death). The decision turned on the question of what was in Anthony's best interests. Rather than retreat in horror from having to determine, quite specifically whether he would be better off alive or dead, the Law Lords were able sensitively and ethically to address the difficult question before them and come to a principled decision. Lord Browne-Wilkinson acknowledged that 'behind the law lie moral, ethical, medical and practical issues of fundamental importance.'[53] Lord Mustill acknowledged the 'deep moral issue of life and death.'[54] Yet neither they nor their colleagues felt compelled to retreat from these issues. Instead, they faced them square on, asked the difficult questions and determined that yes, in such circumstances, it was in Anthony Bland's best interests to cease the 'life' sustaining treatment. Similarly in the tragic case of *In re J (A minor) (Wardship: Medical Treatment),*[55] three of the Law Lords were able to determine that it was appropriate to cease invasive medical treatment of a severely brain damaged infant. In both of these instances, the law was asked to stand poised at one of the borders of life and cast its eye across that border, and to compare existence with non-existence. The result in both instances was, to put it at its most basic, terminal. Yet, in the case of Alexia Harriton (and others in her position), when there is no suggestion that her life is ended,[56] the judges recoil in horror from the question before them. This opens the obvious question as to why? What is it that gives rise

51. [1993] AC 789.
52. *Ibid*, 789.
53. *Ibid*, 877.
54. *Ibid*, 886.
55. [1990] 3 All ER 930.
56. See *Harriton v Stephens* (2006) 226 CLR 53, [101] per Justice Kirby.

to such a specific reaction? Perhaps the answer lies in the potentially negative implications regarding disabled members of our society.

There is some concern expressed in the judicial discussions of these issues that to categorically find that the children would have been better off if they had never been born into a life of disability serves to undermine the value of the lives of the disabled in our communities. However, in this instance the law is not categorically stating that the life of all disabled individuals is worthless. Rather it is a fact-focussed conclusion. If we consider Alexia in particular, her mother recognised that her unborn child was potentially at risk. She sought professional assistance and guidance with the clear intention of termination if she had been exposed to the rubella virus. She had exercised her reproductive autonomy and knew what avenue she was going to take if indeed she had been so exposed. The rights and wrongs of abortion are beyond the scope of this discussion: it is sufficient to note that her choice was a legally and socially accepted one. Yet, as a direct result of the failure of a trusted healthcare professional to act in accordance with the standards of his own profession, she found herself in the position of having a profoundly disabled child. Alexia Harriton lives a life of pain and discomfort and has some very specific medical needs, all of which come at a cost. She is not saying that her life is worthless, nor is she claiming that she ought now be 'put out of her misery.' Rather, she is saying 'I exist', 'I am in discomfort' and 'I need assistance." This assistance is not being sought from a random doctor or other individual. It is most specifically being sought from someone who failed to meet a duty that is grounded in ethics, law and medicine.

If the law is so concerned with taking care not to differentiate between the disabled and the healthy members of society, why did the House of Lords in *McFarlane v Tayside Health Board* [2000] 2 AC 59 find it essential to point out not less than fifty-five times that the child was healthy,[57] and the High Court in *Cattanach* use the phrase 'healthy child' sixty-nine times? Clearly, there is a reason for highlighting the health (or not) of the particular child. Similarly, the three States that have enacted legislation limiting recovery for 'wrongful birth' cases either refer to a healthy child and ordinary costs or exclude additional costs arising from a disability.[58] Clearly, there is some recognition that a life with a disability can be bur-

57. This question was raised by Laura C Hoyona, 'Misconceptions about Wrongful Conception,' in *Modern Law Review*, 65 (2002): 883.

58. Refer *Civil Liability Act 2002* (NSW), s 71 *Civil Liability Act 2003* (Qld), ss 49A and 49B and *Civil Liability Act 1936* (SA), s 67.

densome, one which requires specific recognition and support. This logic was taken one step further by Morris and Saintier when they suggested that the 'tolerance of selective treatment and abortion reflects an acceptance that a disabled life is an impaired life and in some cases is so impaired as to make survival undesirable.'[59]

Thus in contexts outside of the cases before us, the law has drawn that line in the sand and acknowledged that life is not a universal blessing. How then can this acknowledgement be framed so as to provide recompense for those who come before the courts with a 'wrongful birth' or 'wrongful life' claim?

The way forward

The first step is a simple one: remove the emotive labels and lift the judicial eyes from the question of life and sanctity of life. Ask instead: Is one individual in a worse position than they would have been in the absence of the negligence of another? If the answer is yes, then surely recompense sits comfortably within the existing negligence framework. The problem with the current focus is that there is a limit placed upon the ability of the law to address the complex questions of wrongful life/birth. As it stands, the loss is viewed as being the life, even though neither the parents nor the children have claimed that the life itself is the loss. The true loss can be found in the removal of choice, or the denial of choice. In both circumstances the parents have exercised their reproductive choice, the mother in particular has decided that she will not be pregnant (in wrongful life cases) and yet the negligence of the doctors has denied them this exercise of choice. The loss of a right to make such a significant life choice is indeed a loss. The life of the child is not at issue. What ought to be at issue is the autonomy of the parents, the basic right to shape one's own future and set out the path for the journey of that particular family. And it is that right which is denied.

The way forward is, therefore, a shifting of the enquiry and a focus on the real issues. Allow the law to step out from behind the barriers erected on poorly formed ethical and moral foundations. Erect a new enquiry on the firm foundation of legal principle. In short, life itself is not the loss, but the additional burdens that come with an unplanned and unex-

59. Anne Morris and Severine Saintier, 'To Be or Not to Be: Is that the Question? Wrongful Life and Misconceptions', in *Medical Law Review*, 11 (2003): 167, 174.

pected or severely disabled child can amount to a loss. Negligence law asks whether one person acted outside of the expected standard of care and subsequently caused the quality of the life of another to be diminished. In both of the circumstances under consideration, the answer to the law's questions is Yes, and this should be acknowledged.

Keeping Watch on the Border

Ian Maddocks

Ian Maddocks
Flinders University of South Australia
Adelaide, Australia

When death comes suddenly, as with a motor vehicle accident or a massive heart attack, there is no interval of approach to allow either consideration of what has occurred or preparation for what comes next. The border between life and death appears as a single separating fence; the transition through it is swift and final.

Every death can be assigned a defined moment when life is proclaimed extinct, certified by the doctor and noted by the clock, but these days the greater number of deaths are not sudden. They follow a progression of decline extending over days, months or years. An individual diagnosed with potentially fatal illness enters a borderland that extends between life and death. That borderland, a place of interval on the edge of life's familiarity, is an area of new experience. Like the border marches[1] of old, where warlords engaged in repeated conflict, it is a fringe region that can be dangerous, bewildering, and scary. Its unfamiliar territory is filled with new relationships with doctors and hospitals, bringing new vocabularies of diagnosis and therapy, and—often—new discomforts.

The details of experience for the person who is entering those border marches will depend partly on the disease that is edging him on, and its

1. 'Marches' is an archaic term, but one that suits my purpose, referring to territory in dispute, lying between lordly domains and in constant contention.

stage of advance, but the details cannot be anticipated with any certainty. The border-dweller will encounter physical, emotional and spiritual challenges that are prone to vary and change day by day, even hour by hour. He is now a 'patient', and he and those who give him close support must now live with uncertainty, learning to take things as they come.

The threshold

The gateway to the borderland is framed by the structure of diagnosis. Commonly there is a disease recognised as serious, with the capacity to prove fatal. Modern bills of mortality indicate that nearly two-thirds of Australians die from heart disease or cancer. There are differences between those two major killers. For heart disease, there are multiple treatments, surgical and medical: a coronary artery bypass operation or an intra-arterial stent, drug control of hypertension or of cardiac failure. These interventions offer opportunity for a continuation of daily life, and the chance of prolonged survival. The move into the border area is arrested, albeit with some limitation of function and the need for repeated medical review and reassessment of treatment.

Cancer carries the threat of a more inexorable course. Its progress may be stalled and occasionally halted by surgery, chemotherapy or radiotherapy, but cancer will commonly recur, or appear in another site. Then it may prove progressively less amenable to treatment, eroding well-being and comfort with increasing symptoms of pain, nausea, weakness or confusion. Cancer is the most feared cause of death. It is the primary concern of the relatively new medical specialty that I have professed for the past twenty years—palliative care. It is cancer that occupies pride of place in the border marchers.

Resisting entry into the borders

Patient and family responses to the diagnosis of cancer are commonly determined and optimistic—a resolve to fight this thing. 'Think positively' is the mantra shared, and whatever rituals of diet, meditation, or 'natural' supplements are suggested by friends or the worldwide web may be embraced to complement the conventional measures directed against the cancer by medical advisers.

The central medical figure is now the oncologist. From his desk and day-therapy centre, the conventional part of the fight is managed, colleagues in radiotherapy and surgery being called in for consultation and expertise as is seen appropriate.

The origins and natural history of cancer are gradually being revealed as highly complex, with multiple genetic factors, environmental exposures and life style factors contributing to highly variable stories of how a particular cancer may behave in one person or another, or be affected by the administration of one chemotherapy drug or another. A common diagnosis, say, of breast cancer, will be assessed for its cellular characteristics following biopsy or surgery, its genetic or chemical markers, whether it has spread beyond the breast and to which sites. A best judgment will be made concerning which combination of chemotherapy drugs and radiotherapy will give an optimal response in terms of falling marker levels, regression of cancer deposits and patient well-being. Treatments for cancer have a variable capacity to cause symptoms through their own effect on the vulnerable rapidly dividing cells in other tissues. Anaemia or sepsis may follow suppression of bone marrow; nausea and diarrhoea from damage to the cells lining the bowel, peripheral nerves may fail with numbness, weakness or pain.

It is not an easy time. The confident, attentive support of the oncologist will be very important in encouraging continuation of treatments that can cause distress, and a close relationship builds, marked by repeated visits, frequent questions about cancer markers, gifts left on the doctor's desk. The oncologist needs this support. Inflicting distress in the interests of a better future is demanding, and there is much to admire in the pas-de-deux that doctor and patient dance through at this time. The patient demonstrates resilience and bravery while the doctor remains encouraging, taking heart from small gains, researching newer therapies to test, coping with disappointment when the cancer breaks loose in a relapse that calls for a different set of drugs.

The re-appearance of the cancer is often more a threat to the patient than was the first diagnosis. Relapse means that cure is unlikely and further spread may occur. It also marks a more definite step into those badlands, the border marches. Newer drugs will be tried, and there may be further response with renewed optimism, but the usual outcome will be no more than a temporary halt in the progression of the disease, and the beginning of a re-orientation to face life now to be lived within the border.

Journeying within the border

There is considerable variation in how an individual may anticipate or prepare for the journey into and through the border. A marker of change in approach may be a suggestion of referral to palliative care —a request for opinion and management by a team whose focus is care rather than cure, relief of discomfort rather than reversal of pathology. Procrastination is common in the face of this suggestion, and may affect the oncologist—'He's not ready for you yet!'—as well as the patient and family—'This means you are giving up on me?' Increasingly, however, the value of skilled control of symptoms and the regular support with services that encourage comfort and continued function in the face of progressive deterioration is widely recognised, and early referrals to palliative care have become more common, often made during continuing therapy for the cancer.

New questions will be raised. 'How long have I got?' 'What will it be like?' 'Will I have much pain?' Discomforts are more likely at this stage, but their detail cannot be anticipated—everyone is different, and things change repeatedly. Pain, usually the most feared of discomforts, is often relatively easy to address effectively. More difficult is the weakness and tiredness that leads to dependency on others for help with simple actions such as showering or toileting, or a persistent nausea that denies any pleasure from eating.

Dylan Thomas' famous lines, 'Rage, rage, against the dying of the light', sometimes characterise patient responses at such times, and there may be withdrawal and depression, a feeling of being cheated in life, a resentment and bitterness. More often, however, there is a quiet acceptance of a difficult situation, and a willingness to work with caring palliative care staff, trained to help the patient achieve small victories of comfort and occasional pleasure. The patience, courage and serenity that many patients demonstrate to advantage in the terminal phase of illness are compelling testimonies to the human spirit, and helpful, even inspiring, to observers, family and staff. Open sharing of the realities of prognosis and discomfort allow quite cheerful exchanges.

If the final time can be managed at home, that will often prove to be the best of journeys. To offer supervision of care at home is a great privilege and a major source of professional satisfaction. When community nursing services can adequately meet the patient's professional care needs, family members are able to focus on the loving support that they alone can give, and accept an ownership of this important life passage. Encouraging close family and friends to find roles by the bedside reduces their sense of impotence, and brings a new confidence. They may offer regular fluids, provide mouth care, review (and record) personal history, choose music or read poetry or scripture, and sometimes pray together. Open religious expression is not common in the secular world of medicine. However, the ability of a staff person to wait, to stay, to touch and to listen can create a unique sense of connection that leads both patient and professional to feel a sense of awe and a presence beyond themselves. It does not need to be labelled or named, but could be called 'spiritual'. Extending interest and giving time to the wider family can help assuage the grief they are already experiencing and must anticipate.

Can't it be quicker?

Control is an important component of well-being, but individual control is commonly eroded for the patient who is receiving medical care. Many accept this, with a frequent patient response being 'We'll do whatever you say, doctor'. Terminal illness can be prolonged, boring and uncomfortable. Waiting for the next morphine injection or assistance to the toilet will seem demeaning and undignified. Not surprisingly, many patients will ask about how it might be possible to hasten the inevitable: 'Allow me at least some small measure of control; I want out.'

Usually, in my experience, this is not an ideological statement building from long-standing advocacy for euthanasia, but a response to a feeling of powerlessness, and of being a nuisance and an expense to family and society.

The law does not allow me, as a physician, to end life as a deliberate act, but I may withdraw unnecessary or intrusive interventions at the patient's request, even if an end to life is thereby accelerated. I can cease artificial feeding, I can increase medication for pain or anxiety or restlessness. Being sleepier helps the patient to pass the long day, and I feel comfortable about adding additional sedation for a dependent uncomfortable patient. An open negotiation with patient and family about what seems sensible at this stage is usually possible, and working together offers a renewed sense of control.

Euthanasia

With the increasing numbers of frail elderly people in our society, and greater proportions of them demented as survival ages creep up, it seems to me inevitable that calls for some way of assisting death will continue. This is a huge challenge to any society. As doctors, we are asked to be beneficent—to do good and avoid doing harm. Can it be good to effect an end to life by deliberate intent? Should individual autonomy—that sense of control—over-ride our understanding of 'the good'. 'I had no say about coming into this world', remarked one vigorous elderly Dutch doctor, 'I certainly want some say in how and when I leave it.' The Dutch have allowed this; given certain pre-conditions, a doctor can respond to a competent request and administer a fatal dose. In Switzerland, a doctor can prescribe the drugs that a patient will use to commit suicide.

I do not approach this issue with a religious conviction that life is sacred and is to be protected at all costs. Sometimes it seems entirely logical and sensible that a damaged and difficult life close to inevitable death should be allowed to terminate on demand. But I recognise the many complexities: defining suffering and the extent to which it may be classed as 'unbearable', allowing a change of mind, making decisions for an incompetent person, sorting through the tensions and disagreements within families, understanding the uncertainties of prognosis.

I advocate a cautious approach and sufficient time for further consideration and debate, hoping that advocates of euthanasia legislation will be fully aware of the complexities of this issue, mindful of what can already be done, within the law, to smooth the final journey of a dying person, and respectful of the wonder of life and the mystery of death. I hope that we will not be left with clever and precise laws that, while designed to meet the best interests of the individual and of society, encourage desperate action.

Keeping watch

Working in palliative care for over twenty years has been a rich personal experience. There are few medical triumphs to celebrate, but many human individual triumphs to recall. People say it must be difficult, but the medical side is relatively straightforward. The symptoms to be addressed are few and they need to be addressed flexibly and experimentally, changing progressively until a regimen is found that works well enough. There are no 'right answers'. Families are responsive and grateful, and one commonly feels useful. There is an enormous sense of privilege inherent in the opportunity of working with families who must face the crisis of death so closely.

Does my work lead me to think about death? Of course, since I confront its reality daily, but it remains the great unknown, and I touch it tentatively, with a sense of awe and agnosticism. What is beyond the border I cannot know, and know I may never know.

Many of those for whom I offer care are well past their best; they cannot display in their weakened, confused or unresponsive state the personality that others have loved and admired. Only at a funeral will I hear of their many achievements, of winsome personality and loving relationships. Funerals in Australia have changed; they are less often religious ceremonies, more often celebrations with slide displays, jokes, and selective appreciations of good times delivered by mates or children. There is less awe, less ceremony, less homage to the divine, but still there is sadness and some mystery.

Even non-believers will wonder about an after-life, will hope to meet departed loved ones again somehow. It seems an almost a universal human need to frame some concept of life continuing after death, and I respect that, without being able to frame any certainty for myself. Traditional Christian images of heaven, Muslim descriptions of paradise or Asian hopes of reincarnation all lack detail, and are portrayed as often in cartoon and joke as in serious consideration, yet they still remain latent and receive notice.

For six years I lived in a Papuan village where it was felt that the spirits of departed family members stayed close to the house and watched over the lives of their descendants, interfering as they saw fit when behaviour was not respectful of tradition or when anger or wrongdoing was observed. I find this as attractive a hope as any for a life after death. I would quite like to remain around as an interfering spirit, but I have no assurance that my wish will be fulfilled.

Interface Vol 13 1&2/2010

Theological Foundations for Palliative Care in End-Stage Dementia

Rosalie Hudson

Rosalie Hudson
University of Melbourne
Melbourne, Australia

What kind of 'problem'?

> As TS Eliot once remarked, there are two kinds of problems in life. One kind requires the question, what are we going to do about it? The other calls for different questions: What does it mean? How does one relate to it?'[1]

Many certainly view dementia as a problem defying any solution; others see the only solution as dispensing with the 'dementia sufferers'. In his well-publicised remarks about people with dementia in nursing homes, former governor general of Australia, Bill Hayden, stated, 'succeeding generations deserve to be disencumbered of some unproductive burdens'.[2] Sadly, the vocabulary of many health professionals echoes this repugnance towards dementia and dependency: 'Shoot me if I ever get like that!' Baroness Warnock, influential medical ethics expert in the UK, takes the concept

1. Carole Stoneking, 'Modernity: The Social Construction of Aging', in *Growing Old in Christ*, edited by Stanley Hauerwas, Carole Stoneking, Keith Meador, David Cloutier (Grand Rapids, Michigan: Eerdmans, 2003), 63–89.
2. William Hayden, 'Right to Make Choices: Part of Liberal Humanism', in *The Age* (23 June 1995): 15.

further by claiming (in 2008) that 'dementia sufferers should consider ending their lives through euthanasia because of the strain they put on their families and public services'. She also expresses the hope that people will soon be 'licensed to put others down' if they are unable to look after themselves. [3]

Since the Enlightenment, ageing is perceived as a scientific problem ripe for a technical solution; the dream is of a society freed from the vicissitudes of disease and old age. Dementia remains one of the most mysterious maladies mainly because, thus far, it is not amenable to cure. Dementia is one of the fastest growing sources of disease burden in Australia; it is estimated there will be 1.13 million Australians with dementia by mid-century.[4] These statistics are considered less than representative of the real numbers, given that death certificates grossly under-report dementia as the cause of death. Further analysis suggests that 'the number of people with dementia will be 25% higher by mid century than predicted in 2003'.[5]

On a more hopeful plane, people with end-stage dementia now fit the criteria for palliative care, which is 'an approach that improves the quality of life of patients and their families facing the problems associated with life-threatening illness . . .'[6] No longer dependent either on a diagnosis of cancer or on a calculated prognosis, palliative care now applies to chronic disease and is applicable early in the course of illness.

Having set this scene for a discussion on palliative care in end-stage dementia, it is clear that the traditional bio-medical paradigm does not adequately address this relatively recent phenomenon. 'The bio-medical paradigm is not hermeneutically nor philosophically equipped to explore and create new dimensions for understanding the meaning of growing and being old.'[7] Similarly, Seeber asks, 'Why shouldn't gerontology lead the academic enterprise away from the ever-splintering precipice of enquiry toward a more holistic and perhaps more rigorous anthropology

---

3. Martin Beckford, 'Baroness Warnock: dementia sufferers may have a "duty to die"' at<www.telegraph.co.uk/news/uknews/2983652/ Baroness-Warnock-Dementia-sufferers-may-have-a-duty-to-die. html?source=EMC-new_19092008>. Accessed 1 January 2009.
4. Alzheimer's Australia, *The Dementia Epidemic: Economic Impact and Positive Solutions for Australia* (Canberra: Access Economics Pty Ltd, 2009), 6.
5. Alzheimer's Australia, *Dementia Estimates and Projections: Australian States and Territories* (Canberra: Access Economics Pty Ltd, 2005), i.
6. World Health Organisation, 'WHO definition of palliative care', www.who.in/cancer/palliative/definition/en/. Accessed 1 January 2009.
7. Melvin Kimble, 'Beyond the Biomedical Paradigm: Generating a Spiritual Vision of Aging', in *Journal of Religious Gerontology*, 12/3-4, (2001): 31–41.

and theology of life?'[8] There is a growing awareness that an exclusive focus on empirical science is not sufficient to cover issues of life's meaning, particularly at life's end. Different questions are therefore called for. What does it mean to address the 'problem' of dementia from the perspective of a theological understanding of *person*? How can the principles of palliative care apply in this context?

In the presence of death, other questions of meaning arise. What does dying mean to persons with end-stage dementia who are seemingly unable to articulate their hopes or fears? How do the palliative care principles of on 'impeccable assessment and treatment of pain and other problems'[9] apply to persons unable to describe their symptoms? How are their spiritual needs addressed when they cannot distinguish between the chaplain and the cook? How are the means of grace, particularly in the eucharistic ritual, received by a person who has 'forgotten' how to swallow?

This chapter will recall the foundations of palliative care in order to highlight the nature of 'whole person' care. It will show that the earliest and most profound understanding of the human person comes from fourth century Christian theology. The aim of the chapter is to address questions of meaning and to show how palliative care can be related to end-stage dementia in such a way that health professionals are offered encouragement, and those dying with dementia are given the best available care. The chapter includes references to classical and contemporary literature, some scenarios from direct experience, recommendations for change and some priorities for further education. The conclusion is drawn that, given the relevant access to contemporary research, together with a reminder of the roots of palliative care, health professionals can offer hope for those with end-stage dementia and for families desperately seeking support.

Questions of meaning

Palliative care does not operate in a vacuum; rather, it is embedded, along with all health care, in the cultural milieu of contemporary society. Dementia, and other chronic illnesses for which there is no cure, is often treated as a problem to be solved by asking what we can do about it. Novelists have given voice to the attitudes of those who believe the best and only solution is to eliminate the sufferers.

8. James Seeber, 'Spiritual Maturity and Wholeness: a Concept Whose Time Has Come', in *Spiritual Maturity in Later Years*, edited by James Seeber (New York: The Haworth Press, 1990), 3.
9. World Health Organisation, 'WHO definition of palliative care.'

Anthony Trollope's futuristic novel, written in 1882 and set in the late twentieth century, describes the 'Fixed Period' as sixty-seven years of age.

> It is self-evident that at sixty-five a man has done all that he is fit to do. He should be troubled no longer with labour, and therefore should be troubled no longer with life.[10]

When reaching this age, all citizens were to be 'deposited' in a special college ('the Necropolis') where they would spend a year or two preparing comfortably for their death which would, of course, be peaceful and dignified with the aid of chloroform. The advantages of the 'Fixed Period' included 'all those benefits that would come to the world from the race of mankind which knew nothing of the debility of old age'.[11] With striking prescience, 'Trollope stripped the veil of sentimentalism from the verdict of rationalist, secular, capitalist culture: old age is irrelevant and burdensome'.[12]

Similarly, the contemporary crime writer, PD James, imagines a future England where human infertility has spread like a plague so that by 2021 no babies have been born for a quarter of a century. She describes the 'Quietus', a ceremony for death with dignity for all those who have reached sixty-seven years of age. All the safeguards are in place, it is purely voluntary, with forms signed in triplicate. This is their passage to freedom: freedom from boredom, freedom from want, freedom from fear. The old people are led to the water's edge, clothed in white and with the band playing 'Abide with me'. They are gently led into low boats filled with weights, quietly to drift and to sink. On one occasion when something goes terribly wrong, the authorities respond, 'That particular Quietus was mismanaged. Things got out of control. I've asked for a report. Appropriate action will be taken against those responsible. The Council notes your concern.' One onlooker had asked, 'I know that all the old people are supposed to be volunteers… But would they want to die if we gave them hope?'[13] Hope is the theme I will return to at the end of the chapter because, novelists notwithstanding, many older people with end-stage dementia (and their

---

10. Anthony Trollope, *The Fixed Period* (London: Penguin Books, 1993/1882), 21.
11. Trollope, *The Fixed Period*, 30.
12. Carole Stoneking, 'Modernity: The Social Construction of Aging', in *Growing Old in Christ*, 81.
13. PD James, *The Children of Men* (London: Faber and Faber, 1992), 56.

families) see no alternative to the despair which leads to the voluntary or involuntary ending of their lives.

The origins of palliative care

One meaning of the verb 'palliate', derived from the Latin for 'cloak',[14] is the covering of all distressing symptoms with a protective cloak of care. Palliative care, at its best, can be an antidote to the despair which comes from the quest for annihilation of the 'problem' of dementia.

In one of her many surveys, Cicely Saunders asked a dying patient what he looked for above all else in those who were caring for him.

> 'For someone to look as if she is trying to understand me' . . . Mr Martin did not ask for good words, nor indeed even for success in understanding him, but only that someone should care enough to try.[15]

The world of dementia care can indeed be very 'trying' and many attempts to communicate in any meaningful way often seem thwarted. The world of dementia also lends itself, however, to imagination and creativity, and the risky business of appearing foolish and 'non professional' in an attempt to understand the other person's situation. Such was the conclusion of a chaplain visiting a dementia unit.

> There are at least two residents who seem to enjoy my (sometimes off-key) singing. They both have trouble hearing so I have to sing loudly. I know I attract some derisive looks from the staff, but I know what it means to Eric and Ben for the three of us to join in the old hymns. Neither of them can construct a lucid sentence but they sing the hymns, word perfect.

This scenario exemplifies the spirit of hospitality, where host and guest are of one heart and mind and where problem solving gives way to personal communication. It is also reminiscent of the original meaning of hospice

14. *The Australian Concise Oxford Dictionary,* fourth edition, edited by Bruce Moore (Oxford: Oxford University Press, 2004), 1013.
15. Cicely Saunders, *Cicely Saunders: Selected Writings 1958-2004* (Oxford: Oxford University Press, 2006), 82.

and palliative care. Saunders traces the first hospice to the late fourth century of the Common Era when Fabiola, a Roman matron,

> opened her home to pilgrims, the sick and the destitute as a Christian commitment . . . she chose the word 'hospice' which referred to guests or strangers, their hosts and the relationship that developed between them as true hospitality.[16]

Saunders' commitment in founding St Christopher's Hospice in London was to openness where 'the mind, together with the heart and the freedom of the spirit are the three founding principles'.[17] Full scientific rigour that comes from research and a mind open to learning was to be matched with the 'friendship of the heart' which acknowledged the vulnerability of both the patient and the carer.

Tracing these origins gives us a window into the question of *meaning*, rather than trying to find a solution to the *problem*.

What meaning can be attached to the care of people with end-stage dementia?

The questions posed by the novelists above, coupled with the prevalent attitude about the expendability of older people with dementia go to the heart of the other pervasive question about their 'right to life'. Rowan Williams answers: 'Rights belong not to the person who can demonstrate capacity or rationality but to any organism that can be recognised as a human body, at any stage of its organic development'.[18] Williams claims, furthermore, that the idea of irreducible or non-negotiable liberties for human beings has a strong theological basis. Such a basis, he continues,

> takes us away from the more unhelpful aspects of those rights theories that stress the grounding of rights in human dignity but then associate human dignity with a particular set of capacities. The danger of these is that, by trying to identify a list of essential capacities, it becomes possible to identify criteria according to which full claims to human rights may

16. Saunders, *Selected Writings*, 252.
17. *Ibid.*
18. Rowan Williams, 'Faith and Human Rights' at <www.archbishipofcanterbury.org/1780>. Accessed 1 January 2009.

> be granted or withheld. The right of the imperfectly rational person—whether the child or the person with mental disabilities—may be put in question if we stipulate a capacity for reasoned self-consciousness as a condition for acknowledging rights.[19]

To understand one another as communicating beings is, according to Williams, to acknowledge that in our mutuality we each have the gift of communication which is neither dependent on our rationality or our verbal capacity. On this view, the human person can never be regarded as another person's 'property' whose right to exist can be debated. In shared communion with Christ, and in shared obedience, we are present to one another. 'This holds true even for the most inarticulate, or those whose communications are hardest to decode: to put it as vividly as I can, they still have *faces*.'[20] The relevance of this theological understanding for palliative care is that health professionals are encouraged to look beyond the patients' defining characteristics, which are so often catalogued in terms of deficits, to see in the face of the person with dementia the whole person. In other words, to see past the plaques and tangles of the diseased brain, to the person who is uniquely, irreplaceably, and equally made in the image of God. This way of communicating breaks down the barriers of 'us and them' to find a place of true meeting.

In their study of people with Alzheimer's disease, Sabat and Harré found that in order to preserve the self, mutual cooperation with others is needed.

> Thus, if there is a loss of the capacity to present an appropriate self, in many cases the fundamental cause is to be found not in the neurofibrillary tangles and senile plaques in the brains of the sufferers, but in the character of the social interactions and their interpretation that follow in the wake of the symptoms.[21]

Thus, we are given some clues about the location of meaning. If we seek meaning by looking at the person merely from the perspective of their

19. Williams, 'Faith and Human Rights'.
20. *Ibid.*
21. Steven Sabat and Rom Harré, 'The Construction and Deconstruction of Self in Alzheimer's Disease', in *Ageing and Society*, 12 (1992): 44–61.

diseased brain cells, then we will miss the truth, the joy and the spirit of freedom derived from a relational understanding. Meaning is to be found not in each person as an isolated monad, but in mutuality and reciprocity—in the interdependence of our relationships.

> Within a relational understanding of personhood these older persons have been given to us and we to them, each to mediate the grace and presence of Jesus Christ; daring us to believe that we belong to the one community, demonstrating that our relationship with God does not decrease in proportion to our cognitive impairment.[22]

Meaning of person: theological and palliative care origins

Within a relational understanding, our being persons is not dependent on our qualities or capacities, neither can our uniqueness be defined. On this understanding, we cannot claim to know the person with end-stage dementia merely by gathering information about them. That is not to say that individual characteristics are unimportant; rather, we are to see them in a relational context. 'In each person we see not only a part of humanity; we see the whole. This corporate humanity does not detract from the utter uniqueness and unrepeatable nature of each person.'[23] Zizioulas puts it more concisely: 'Thus communion does not threaten personal particularity; it is constitutive of it.'[24]

The true meaning of person is to be found in its theological foundations in the fourth century. Zizioulas claims that 'nobody seems to recognise that, *historically* as well as *existentially*, the concept of the person is indissolubly bound up with theology'.[25] Furthermore, he says:

> Belief in creation *ex nihilo*—biblical faith—thus encounters belief in ontology—Greek faith—to give to human existence and thought its most dear and precious good, the concept of

22. Rosalie Hudson, 'Dementia: the Death of Faith?' In *Interface: a Forum for Theology in the World*, 4/2 (2001): 59–77.
23. Rosalie Hudson, 'Dementia and Personhood: a Living Death or Alive in God?' In *Colloquium: the Australian and New Zealand Theological Review*, 36/2 (2004): 123-42.
24. John Zizioulas, 'Human Capacity and Human Incapacity: a Theological Exploration of Personhood', in *Scottish Journal of Theology*, 28 (1975): 401–48.
25. John Zizioulas, *Being as Communion: Studies in Personhood and the Church* (London: Darton, Longman and Todd, 1985), 27.

> the person. This and nothing less than this is what the world owes to Greek patristic theology.[26]

The relational concept of persons in communion drawn from theology also matches the history of palliative care located in the ancient hospices of the fourth century where 'hospes', originally meaning host, was gradually used to refer also to strangers or guests'.[27] In this atmosphere, no individual was seen apart from the community. This is not to undermine the importance of individualised care, tailored to the uniqueness of each hospice patient or nursing home resident, for, as Ferrell states, patient and nurse together form a partnership in which healing is fostered.

> In palliative care nursing, the 'individual' is recognized as a very important part of the healing relationship. The nurse's individual relationship with the patient and family is seen as crucial. This relationship, together with knowledge and skills, is the essence of palliative care nursing and sets it apart from other areas of nursing practice.[28]

The focus on the individual is to be seen also in the context of team work, multidisciplinary focus, and a sense of community. When persons are seen in their communal relationships, no person can be regarded as more, or less, worthy of care than any other person.

Viewed through the bio-medical lens, the person with end-stage dementia might well appear expendable. On the spurious 'quality of life' measure, the person's score might be close to zero. Viewed through the economic lens the same person might well be judged as serving no useful purpose to society. According to orthodox theology, however, the nature of our relationships is grounded not in ourselves, nor in our potential (or lack thereof), but in the communal relationship of the trinitarian God into whose fellowship Christians are called. In this trinitarian drawing near, as David Hart beautifully expresses it, 'there can be no exile'.[29] This is

26. Zizioulas, *Being as Communion,* 65.
27. Saunders, *Selected Writings,* 205.
28. Nessa Coyle, 'Introduction to Palliative Nursing Care', in *Textbook of Palliative Nursing,* edited by Betty Ferrell and Nessa Coyle (Oxford: Oxford University Press, 2006), 7.
29. David Hart, *The Beauty of the Infinite* (Grand Rapids, Michigan: Eerdmans, 2003), 323. See also Rosalie Hudson, 'Orthodox Faith: a Lively Spirit for Older People' in *Ageing and Spirituality Across Faiths and Cultures,* edited by Elizabeth MacKinlay (London and Philadelphia: Jessica Kingsley Publications, 2010), 152-166.

indeed good news for those with end-stage dementia and for their families who often experience abandonment and despair.

While palliative care has now become far more secularised, health professionals who witness to its origins can also reclaim the communal understanding of person, invoking the essence of relationships and life narratives rather than treating dementia as an isolated problem.[30] A relational approach addresses the whole person as more than the sum of their symptoms, takes seriously their unique life story, and invites families to be partners in care.

Quality of life or image of God

We have referred above to the uniqueness of each person made in the image of God. The question often posed is whether this image can be lost? We hear this heartfelt question from family members and carers who talk about the person with dementia as a 'lost soul'. 'She's no longer a person, she's just a shell'; 'there's nobody home' or 'the lights have gone out upstairs'; 'it's like a living death'; 'he's no longer the husband I knew'; 'she's just a breathing corpse'; or, the widow's comment, 'this funeral started for me ten years ago'. These are very real and understandable reactions of those living with the everyday reality of dementia, in some situations for more than a decade. What meaning can be found in the life of this person, seemingly unaware, mute and bedbound? How can we avoid resorting to false consolation and platitudes based on body/soul dualism such as 'his body and brain might be decaying but his spirit is with God'?

The constraints of this chapter do not permit an excursus into the Greek Platonic notion that separates the body from the soul. However, a 'whole person' understanding can be derived from the terms 'ensouled body' and 'embodied soul'.[31] These terms signify our shared life in Christ where the body is not inferior to the spirit, and we are all seen to be in need of healing, bodily and spiritually. On this view, we come as health professionals to care for the person with end-stage dementia not as those

30. For narrative accounts in the context of dementia and palliative care, see Neil Small, Katherine Froggart, Murna Downs, *Living and Dying with Dementia: Dialogues About Palliative Care* (Oxford: Oxford University Press, 2007), and Rosalie Hudson and Margaret O'Connor, *Palliative Care and Aged Care: a Guide to Practice* (Melbourne: Ausmed Publications, 2007), 109–26.

31. Rosalie Hudson, 'Disembodied souls or soul-less bodies: spirituality as fragmentation', in *Journal of Religion, Spirituality and Aging*: 18/2–3, 45–57.

with superior wisdom or power but as those also in need of one another, all of us dependent on God, the transcendent Other. The need for this co-dependence is described by Kitwood.

> The dementia sufferer needs the Other for personhood to be maintained . . . the Other is needed, not to work with growth, but to offset degeneration and fragmentation, and the further the dementing process advances, the greater is the need for that 'person work' . . . the self that is shattered in dementia will not naturally coalesce; the Other is needed to hold the fragments together. As subjectivity breaks apart, so intersubjectivity must take over if personhood is to be maintained.' [32]

When persons are understood to be made in the image of God, all dependent on one another, the 'quality' question is redundant, for it isolates an individual as an object for calculation and classification, rather than seeing a person in relation to other persons.

Non persons

Contrary to any communal understanding, Peter Singer argues that rational capacity is essential to personhood. By this criterion, people with end-stage dementia fail the test. Along with the foetus and the fish, according to Singer, they meet the definition of *non persons.*[33] Such a view not only kills the spirit of relationships with frail older people; it can quickly lead to the involuntary killing of the people themselves. As Swinton argues:

> This leaves us with the rather odd situation wherein human beings can be persons for 60, 70, 80 years, and live under the protection of this particular notion of personhood, only to find themselves living out their final years as non-persons who suddenly (or gradually) become less worthy of moral attention and protection.[34]

---

32. Tom Kitwood and Kathleen Bredin, 'Towards a Theory of Dementia Care: Personhood and Well-being', in *Ageing and Society,* 12 (1992): 269–87.
33. Peter Singer, *Rethinking Life and Death: the Collapse of Our Traditional Ethics* (Melbourne: The Text Publishing Company, 1994), 183.
34. John Swinton, 'Remembering the Person: Theological reflections on God, Personhood and Dementia', in *Ageing, Disability and Spirituality: Addressing the Challenge of*

Similarly, Stephen Post challenges the notion of our 'hypercognitive' culture which sees dementia as an affront to our values.

> Is this really 'life unworthy of life'? Are those who are deeply forgetful mere 'shells' or 'husks' of humanity; does forgetfulness dissolve the autobiographical narrative of our lives?[35]

Does our ability to think really constitute who we are? If we follow the Cartesian dictum, 'I think, therefore I am', how are those with end-stage dementia defined? A theological understanding of the origins of person seriously calls into question any claim to 'non-personhood' and reduces to absurdity any notion that a person can be a non-person.

Whose remembering?

On the question whether we can define persons by their capacity to remember, the Psalmist corrects our perspective and gives us hope: 'How precious to me are thy thoughts, O God, how vast is the sum of them' (Psalm 139:17–18). The psalmist's emphasis is not on our capacity to think about God but on God's overflowing graciousness in remembering us. Waking or sleeping, conscious or unconscious, even in Sheol, the place of forgetfulness and dust, God remembers us.

From a Christian perspective, it is God's remembering of us that sustains us; and that includes those who no longer have the capacity to remember God's remembering of them. However, that does not give us licence to forget the significance of human touch through embodied, close personal presence. In this sense, it is our visiting, our sustaining relationships, together with those of families that nurture and nourish. In the body of Christ, we not only remember whose we are; we are remembered—given new membership.

Keck takes this remembering a step further, by suggesting that we are called by our discipleship not only to 'remember for' those with dementia but to assume responsibility for believing for them. In an age which privileges rationality and autonomy, this might at first glance appear paternalistic. However, within the framework of our communal identity granted through the death and resurrection of Jesus Christ, we are all dependent on one another. Keck explains:

Disability in Later Life, edited by Elizabeth MacKinlay (London and Philadelphia: Jessica Kingsley Publishers, 2008), 22–35.

35. Stephen Post, 'Alzheimer's & Grace', in *First Things* (April 2004): 12–14.

> As the community accepts the responsibility of believing for a newly-baptized infant, so too at the end of life does the church accept this task for those in end-stage dementia . . . Not everyone can bear this plenitude—either as caregiver or a Christian—but, as caregivers strive to sustain the fullness of a person, so should the body of Christ seek to bear the fullness of his work.[36]

Keck reminds us of our own failure to remember; and in failing to remember our own calling to care for one another, we abandon those without the capacity to remember, to further silence and isolation. As those who claim, by faith, to belong to the communion of saints, we are continually reminded that our life is communal; that we are all in need of reconciliation and forgiveness; that we belong to one communion in both this life and the next.

Our calling to 'remember for them' comes to unique expression when the means of grace are offered to those whose life history includes the rituals of the church. The following scenario, described by a chaplain, is one of many stories exemplifying the remarkable response triggered by such rituals.

> An aged lady in an advanced stage of dementia was nearing the end of her life . . . With the progression of her physical condition, she was unable to swallow . . . A few days before she died, I repeated the familiar liturgy for the celebration of holy communion and then proceeded to place a few drops of consecrated wine on her lips . . . Suddenly her eyes opened and her lips moved with a soft 'amen' . . . Memories were revived through words, touch and taste.[37]

Such stories from everyday lived experience seriously call into question the often heard, but patently ignorant 'counsel' from health professionals: 'I wouldn't bother; she won't have a clue what you're doing.' For health professionals, end-stage dementia might not always feature as dramati-

36. David Keck, *Forgetting Whose We Are: Alzheimer's Disease and the Love of God* (Nashville: Abingdon Press, 1996), 91, 134.
37. Noel Schultz, *Forgetting But Not Forgotten: Understanding, Support and Spiritual Care for People with Dementia and Those Who Care for Them* (Adelaide: Open Book Publishers, 2004), 55.

cally as end-stage cancer. While many patients needing palliative care are able to describe their symptoms and show appreciation for the alleviation of pain, and to make rational judgments about their spiritual needs, the person with dementia often lacks the verbal capacity for such response. To neglect their spiritual care is, however, as serious as leaving them in physical pain.

Those of us who have been named Christian by our baptism are called to discipleship. Those who also serve as health professionals or pastors or other carers for people with end-stage dementia have a particular calling to remember.

> As disciples, we are called to remember as God remembers—as concrete, particular, active, other-oriented, present, eucharistic, embodied, life-giving, relationship-constituting, faithful, and reconciling.[38]

This imposes a particular call to understanding what it means to care for a person with end-stage dementia. It is a call daily to enact who and whose we are; to demonstrate in practice our knowledge gained from the best research; and to role model the imperative to care for those who are weak and vulnerable.

Practical considerations

Palliative care practice, incorporating the notion of remembering, calls for new words in our lexicon: commitment, faithfulness, forgiving, and loving. Such sustained relationships require time, will and action. 'As anyone in a nursing home will tell us, not only is it important to be remembered, it is also crucial to be visited.'[39]

In contrast to Keck's emphasis on visiting, there is more than one nursing home in Australia where the injunction is given to families, 'We think it best if people with dementia have no visitors for the first two or three weeks, to allow them to settle in'. Apart from any lack of evidence to validate this 'rule', one can only express deep regret for the suffering imposed on those who have no voice to articulate their longings, and for their imposed isolation.

---

38. M Therese Lysaught, 'Memories, Funerals, and the Communion of Saints: Growing Old and Practices of Remembering', in *Growing Old in Christ*, 294.
39. David Keck, *Forgetting Whose We Are*, 47.

Cicely Saunders was well aware of the importance of *approach*, particularly to those dying of chronic illness, urging nurses and doctors to 'look continually at the patients, not at their need but at their courage, not at their dependence but at their dignity'. Her appeal came from the experience of a hospice patient who said, 'I thought it so strange. Nobody wants to look at me.'[40] Saunders reminds us that, important as our clinical tasks may be, the therapeutic value of human to human encounter is incalculable. For persons with end-stage dementia, these encounters may live only fleetingly in their memories; and while they may not be amenable to recording on a clinical chart, we are in no position to invalidate their worth.

One of the hallmarks of both palliative care and aged care is the mutual setting of goals. It is through comprehensive care planning, in collaboration with family where relevant, that goals are assessed and implemented and the interventions regularly reviewed. It has been established, however, that attention to this extremely important framework of care is often lacking, as evident in the following scenario.

> Mrs A is transferred from her nursing home to the ED (emergency department) of an acute hospital, accompanied by her only family member, a niece. Mrs A is curled up in the foetal position; she has severe osteoarthritis, is severely malnourished, and has several bedsores. She is admitted to hospital with symptoms of end-stage respiratory failure. She also has late stage dementia and is unable to articulate her wishes. The niece appears utterly astonished by the ED doctor's question about advance care planning or established goals of care, stating this question had never been put to her before. In the opinion of the ED staff, Mrs A would benefit more from a palliative approach than from intrusive care, including intubation, in the ICU (intensive care unit). When the options were sensitively outlined to the niece, she had no hesitation in stating, 'Yes, this is exactly what my aunt would prefer.' There was no need for further discussion about resuscitation; the niece was reassured that a palliative approach would include careful attention to any distressing symptoms and that her aunt's comfort would be maintained with judicious use of analgesia. 'Why couldn't they have offered us this in the nursing home?' was the niece's legitimate but unanswered question.

40. Cicely Saunders, *Selected Writings*, 79.

There are, of course, many other scenarios where, by contrast, careful planning is evident in the nursing home and found lacking in the acute ward. The point is made, however, that advance care planning is of the utmost importance for the person with end-stage dementia, and it has been shown that such planning brings satisfaction to families and carers.[41] Best practice suggests that a well conducted meeting with patient/resident and/or family soon after admission to the particular care setting builds trust and confidence and paves the way for the person's wishes to be respected at the time of serious health crisis or death.

Recommendations for change

Recent findings in the US suggest that 'palliative care for nursing home residents with advanced dementia is suboptimal, and encourages use of educational strategies to promote palliative care to these patients'.[42] While some of the following recommendations are perceived to be beyond the capacity of current government resources within Australia, they should remain as priorities for reform. They are also congruent with the changes recommended in the US.

1. Wage parity between aged care nurses and acute care nurses, which acknowledges that while different skills are needed, the former are not inferior to the latter.
2. Increase in the numbers of professional staff in residential aged care, in acknowledgement of the particular gerontological nursing expertise required for optimum care of people with dementia.
3. Increase in the ratio of staff to residents, which allows for validated 'person centred' care to become a reality.
4. Widespread uptake of the government endorsed guidelines for a palliative approach in end-stage dementia.[43]
5. Exploring creative, practical partnerships between palliative care and aged care professionals.

41. Commonwealth of Australia, *Guidelines for a Palliative Approach in Residential Aged Care: Enhanced Version* (Canberra: Australian Government Department of Health and Ageing, 2006), 55–59.
42. Susan Derby and Sean O'Mahony, 'Elderly Patients', in *Textbook of Palliative Nursing*, 637.
43. Commonwealth of Australia, *Guidelines for a Palliative Approach*, 61–2.

Priorities for further education

We should not assume that palliative care health professionals have contemporary knowledge and skills in the care of people with end-stage dementia. Nor should we assume that all aged care workers are aware of contemporary best practice in palliative care. This issue is too important to be left to isolated care contexts. Rather, a partnership of relevant expert health professionals is considered the preferred option.[44] Arising from such research, the following points are offered. They are not intended as a comprehensive list, but represent some broad categories of priorities for further education.

- Understanding the revolution in dementia care, for example the work pioneered by Kitwood[45]
- Focusing on the *person* rather than the diagnosis[46]
- Countering the myth that 'people with dementia don't feel pain'
- Establishing a relationship of trust with family members
- Application of latest research into family carers' needs[47]
- Comprehensive understanding of impeccable symptom management
- Use of relevant guidelines for all aspects of care
- Referral to specialist consultants, such as psycho-geriatrician, where necessary
- Careful assessment of spiritual and cultural needs, based on thorough knowledge of the person's background, beliefs and values.

Conclusion: a hopeful future

The Christian hope takes us, eschatologically, beyond history, even beyond our own experience of ageing and dying. Christian hope takes us beyond our fate or our fortune or our forgetfulness. We therefore hope, not according to our individual capacity, but in communion with all the saints through the ages.

---

44. Sonia Allen, Ysanne Chapman, Margaret O'Connor, Karen Frances, 'The evolution of palliative care and the relevance to residential aged care: understanding the past to inform the future', in *Collegian,* 15/4 (2008): 165–71.
45. Tom Kitwood, *The New Culture of Dementia Care* (London: Hawker Publications, 1995).
46. Tom Kitwood, *Dementia Reconsidered: the Person Comes First* (Buckingham Philadelphia: Open University Press, 1997).
47. Peter Hudson and Sheila Payne (editors), *Family Carers in Palliative Care: a Guide For Health and Social Care Professionals* (Oxford: Oxford University Press, 2008).

Hope, in this context, is neither constrained by cheerful optimism, nor by frenetic attempts to keep old age and death at bay. Finitude need not imply failure to thrive or survive; rather, our finitude constitutes a sure and certain sign of freedom, promise and hope. Lewis warns against phony cheerfulness that merely 'hopes for the best' or, with fingers crossed, hopes to 'just get by'. Rather, he sees in the Christian hope the miracle of death's sting being removed forever.

> If we allow our words, our manner, our status or professionalism, or—deadliest of all in certain circumstances—our breezy faith and heroic confidence, to distance us from those who doubt and stumble, weep and hurt, we surely betray the God of the cross and of the grave, obscuring the truth that their vexation is but a shadow of God's own anger, and their tears an earthly drop in the ocean of heavenly grief.[48]

By the warmth of our personal presence, through the hope of the Christian gospel of death and resurrection, we can claim with confidence that, even in death and beyond, and together with those whose memories have faded, God never fails to remember us.

The aim of this chapter has been to offer some Christian theological foundations for palliative care in end-stage dementia. In drawing on the historical roots of palliative care and tracing the theological understanding of 'person', a countercultural approach is offered. It is to be hoped, in the very best sense of the word, that such an approach provides a realistic, practical framework for care. We are called, weak and strong, living and dying, with impaired or intact cognition, to be persons in relation, for the sake of our common humanity.

48. Alan Lewis, 'Death, Dying and Pastoral Context', in *Insights*, 110 (Fall 1994): 7–18.

Interface Vol 13 1&2/2010

Is it *Always* Good to be Alive?

Gerald Gleeson

Gerald Gleeson
Catholic Institute of Sydney
Sydney, Australia

When asked how he was, the retired archbishop was wont to say, 'Not bad, when you consider the alternative.' Notwithstanding the infirmities of old age—and his presumed faith in a next life—the archbishop wanted to go on living. His sentiment would be understood and shared by most human beings, even in their darkest moments. But is it *always* good to be alive? Or are there situations in which we could reasonably conclude that someone, perhaps oneself, would be 'better off dead'? This is a fundamental philosophical question behind current ethical debates about euthanasia and abortion. In this chapter I explore contrasting philosophical approaches to answering this question and defend that approach which relies on the perspective of human beings as 'acting subjects'.

I begin by recalling people whose situations lead some people to think it would be better for them not to be alive: a terminally ill person, with a poor 'quality of life' and the prospect of a lingering death; an accident victim with a severe brain injury and little or no prospect of recovery (or whose prospects of recovery, if at all, would be in 'a vegetative state');[1]

1. The National Health and Medical Research Council has rightly rejected the disparaging connotations of the term 'vegetative', and recommends that we speak of 'post-coma unresponsiveness'; see *Ethical Guidelines For The Care Of People In Post-Coma Unresponsiveness (Vegetative State) Or A Minimally Responsive State* (Australian Government: NHMRC, 2008).

a severely disabled new born child with a short life expectancy, largely occupied with medical procedures, who will never speak or otherwise communicate; an 'unwanted' child whom an impoverished mother feels unable to care for; a parent who lives to see a son disgraced and convicted of heinous crimes. Should we say of the people in these situations that it is good for them just to be alive, rather than dead, or should these and similar cases lead us to conclude that while it is *generally* good to be alive, there are times when being alive ceases to be good for a person, so that—as the colloquial phrase has it—that person would be 'better off dead'?

As with so-called 'wrongful birth' claims, it is of course paradoxical to say that it is bad for someone to be alive. Even if life could be bad for person, how could not being alive be good for a person, if there is no (longer) someone for whom it is good? Reviewing the situations above, however, we should note that there are ways of understanding them that avoid paradox because they do not involve the precise thought that a person would be better off dead. Thus: we could simply hope that a person's terminal illness will not be painfully drawn out; we could regard it a blessing that, as a consequence of death, a brain injured accident victim is spared a lifetime of severe disability; we could wisely judge that extraordinary, life-saving interventions not be imposed on a severely disabled new born child, thereby prolonging the burdens of their short life; we could be grateful that, should a natural miscarriage occur, difficulties for both mother and child are avoided; and we can be comforted by the thought that a deceased parent never knew of their son's disgrace.

Each of these responses is consistent with the judgment that (as I will argue), although death is always bad for a person who dies insofar as life is ended, death may nonetheless have good side-effects for which we may be grateful. There is no paradox in what is commonly experienced on the death of a loved one: both sadness at the ending of their life along with relief that other evils such as prolonged suffering or disability have been precluded.

Yet, even if there are more thoughtful approaches to difficult situations that avoid the claim that a person would be better off dead, we have still not addressed the properly *ethical* question about what we may or should *do* in relation to people in these situations. If it is permissible to hope that a person's dying will not be drawn out, is it also permissible to deliberately bring about their death? Does the reasonable hope that a person will never experience certain sufferings make it right to end their life in order to prevent those sufferings? Ethics is about what we may or ought *to do* (or *not do*), and about the kind of people we become as a result of our actions. It is one thing to recognise the good and bad things that happen in life, it is quite another thing to judge what are the good or bad things we may or ought to do in relation to what happens.[2]

The consequentialist perspective

In taking up the properly ethical question about what we may or ought to do in relation to the good of being alive, the perspective we adopt is crucial. The most obvious, because culturally dominant, perspective is that associated with utilitarianism or, more generally, 'consequentialism'. The different versions of consequentialism rely on *an observer's* perspective (what Peter Singer, following Henry Sidgwick calls 'the view of the universe'), and from this 'god's eye' perspective evaluating 'states of affairs' as good or bad.[3] Different versions of consequentialism offer different accounts of what constitutes a good or bad state of affairs (pleasure/pain, satisfaction/frustration of one's desires or interests, and so on); yet, however good and bad states of affairs are measured, the common ethical rule in consequentialism is that our actions ought, overall, to maximise good states of affairs and minimise bad states of affairs. From such a perspective it may not always be good to be alive, since the *prima facie* good of just being alive can be offset (discounted, outweighed) by the associated bad states of affairs. In other words, for the consequentialist, the state of being alive is just one among many states of affairs that need to be assessed in determining what we ought to do, in determining what maximally good state of affairs we ought to bring about.

Consequentialist philosophers and theologians often claim that the rightness of their approach is virtually self-evident. What else ought we to do, they ask, other than to maximise good states of affairs (or personal happiness, or the satisfaction of individual interests and so on)?[4] How could it be right simply to do nothing but stand by and watch a person's extended terminal suffering, or prolonged unresponsive 'life', or struggle with grave disabilities, or birth in untoward circumstances? If we reason-

2. See Peter Geach, *God and the Soul* (London: Routledge & Kegan Paul, 1969), 120–21.
3. See, for example, Peter Singer, *How are we to live?* (East Melbourne: Text Publishing Co, 1993), 219–35.
4. For a defence of the merits of consequentialism see, for example, Phillip Pettit, 'Consequentialism', in Peter Singer, editor, *A Companion to Ethics* (Oxford: Blackwell, 1993), 230–40.

ably judge that someone would be better off dead, then surely we ought to bite the bullet and purposefully end their lives—unless, of course, the good of doing so would be offset by other evils, such as the person's preference to go on living, or the sorrow of their loved ones.

At this point the well-known objections to consequentialism arise. First, there is the paradox already noted: however it may be with other goods, the good of just being alive is fundamental; without life, there is no person to have pleasures or interests or satisfactions. We may say of the good of life what one seminal utilitarian said of freedom, that it should not enter the calculation of goods and evils. Thus JS Mill held that no one could rightly sell themselves into slavery.[5] As Elizabeth Anscombe noted in her ground breaking essay, 'Modern Moral Philosophy', Mill did not count as a pure consequentialist.[6] Mill did not think that *all* ethical judgments could be reduced to judgments about good and bad states of affairs, since he thought there were some actions 'of a class' which 'it would be unworthy of an intelligent agent not to be consciously aware . . . would be generally injurious.'[7] Traditionally, the killing of innocent human beings has been one such class of actions, called 'murder', the prohibition of which is at the heart of what makes it possible for people to live together in society. Today, however, even Mill's somewhat restricted utilitarianism has given way to an unrestricted consequentialism in which there are no absolute moral prohibitions.

Yet even if just being alive could be counted among the various goods and evils in the consequentialist calculus, the second well-known objection to consequentialism concerns the incommen-surability of the different goods open to us. The consequentialist must assume that there is a common measure for goodness, and hence that—at base—there is only one kind of good to which all other goods are reducible. Such 'monism' about the good is implausible. It is because there is no common standard, or super-value, by which to measure or calculate the goodness of diverse states of affairs that we face the ubiquitous problem of how to 'reconcile' the claims of the many different goods we are engaged with.[8] Thus, to have

---

5. JS Mill, 'On Liberty', Chapter 5 of *Utilitarianism, On Liberty, Essay on Bentham* (London: Collins/Fontana, 1971), 235, 6.
6. GEM Anscombe, 'Modern Moral Philosophy', in her *Collected Papers, Volume 3* (Oxford: Blackwell, 1981), 26–42.
7. JS Mill, 'Utilitarianism', Chapter 2 in op cit, 270. Anscombe argues that Mill's account of such general prohibitions was, nonetheless, incoherent—'stupid' in her words—because he lacked an account of how 'classes of action' should be described.
8. See TDJ Chappell, *Understanding Human Goods—A Theory of Ethics* (Edinburgh:

lost the power of one's limbs is obviously a bad state of affairs, yet many people live satisfactory lives despite being reliant on a wheelchair or on the care of other people. For them, the good of being alive is clearly preferable to the disabilities they endure. *Who* is to say which is the better state of affairs—life with disability or no life at all? The incommensurability problem thus raises two questions. First, is there a rational way of measuring and trading off diverse goods and bads, and secondly, if there is, *who* is to do the measuring and trading?

The autonomy perspective

At this point, the most appealing move is to the person concerned as the best judge of what's good for them. The idea is to settle the trading problem by invoking a privileged trader, who is not a detached observer, but a conscious, experiencing subject. The incommensurability problem, it might be said, only arises if one thinks in the abstract, from the perspective of no one in particular. In the abstract, *being alive* and *being able to walk and talk* might be incommensurable, like apples and aeroplanes, different kinds of goods. In any particular case, however, the individual concerned may well be able to compare for themselves the good of being alive with the evil of being unable to walk and talk. For some, the disabilities will outweigh continuing to live: 'I would rather be dead than to live like this', they might say. For others, just being alive and being cared for by loved ones might be a preferable good, so that they are willing to put up with their disabilities: 'I have no wish to die', they might say, 'even though my life is so restricted.'[9] On this approach, there is no general answer to the question whether it is always good to be alive—that is something for individuals to judge for themselves.

This approach highlights personal autonomy as the chief ethical value, and autonomy is often taken as the sole basis for 'advance directives' in which people indicate how they wish to be treated should they cease to be competent decision makers. It is also the basis for arguments in support of legalised voluntary euthanasia (and for a woman's right to control her body, and thereby the life of the unborn child she carries). Arguments for voluntary euthanasia commonly emphasise the pain and suffering that terminally ill patients want to avoid. However, when the availability of

---

Edinburgh University Press, 1998), 21.

9. Autonomy also figures in the 'preference satisfaction' version of utilitarianism associated with Peter Singer.

palliative care is noted, it becomes apparent that what advocates of euthanasia really want is control over their lives. The demand is for the legal right to end one's life whenever one has had enough—by whatever standards one wishes to measure this!

The autonomy perspective is half-right: ethics should be undertaken from the perspective of the agent concerned. However, the human agent is not simply a locus of autonomous choices. Choice or autonomy cannot be the sole basis of ethical evaluation because actions do not become good or right merely because I choose them. If autonomous choice alone made actions right and valuable, then right and value would be trivialised.[10] Autonomous choice presupposes what Charles Taylor calls horizons of intelligibility and value that make choices meaningful, horizons that derive from the nature of reality, from sources beyond the choosing self. Human beings possess a specifically human nature that constitutes objective parameters for good and bad choices.

This point is clearly to be seen in debates about voluntary euthanasia, whose advocates normally propose legal 'safeguards' in relation to a patient's choice: for example, that the patient be terminally ill, not depressed, fully informed, and so on. The irony is that in proposing these 'safeguards' the advocates of voluntary euthanasia admit that choice alone is not a sufficient justification. It is not enough for someone merely to request euthanasia; the request has to meet some objective criteria if it is to be a valid (or truly 'autonomous') choice. The irony intensifies, however, once we notice that *either* these criteria become the true justification for euthanasia (and patient request drops out—for why should incompetent patients be denied the good of euthanasia?) *or* these criteria cease to be necessary at all (and patient request alone is sufficient—for why should euthanasia be denied to the depressed or those who are not terminally ill?).[11]

The autonomy perspective rightly emphasises the freedom of the acting person, but it typically fails to ask what human freedom is for.[12] In the remainder of this essay I respond to the question whether it is always good to be alive from the perspective of an ethics that recognises the objectivities of human existence as parameters for the exercise of human agency.

10. Charles Taylor, *The Ethics of Authenticity* (Cambridge, MA: Harvard University Press, 1992), Chapter 4.
11. Hence the many studies reporting the slide from voluntary to non-voluntary euthanasia in those jurisdictions which have legal provision for euthanasia.
12. This question is at the heart of Pope John Paul II's encyclical, *Veritatis Splendor* [*The Splendour of the Truth*] (Homebush: St Pauls, 1993).

Ethics from the perspective of the acting human subject

The first-person perspective of the agent contrasts with the detached, 'god's-eye' view of an observer. Whereas an observer *thinks about* what is good or bad in the world, an agent faces *choices* about what it would be good or bad to do. Ethics is concerned not so much with good and bad states of affairs, but with the goodness or badness of what we do in relation to those states of affairs. As agents we are engaged with goods—they motivate, and give intelligible point to, our actions. And since there are many goods, we face the problem of practical (rather than theoretical) rationality in dealing with the competing demands of the various goods open to us.[13] That something might be good for me in some sense is not a sufficient ethical justification for me to pursue that good. Ethical justification of my actions depends on several factors: on what is good or bad for me and others, and—more crucially—on what my actions mean, what values they instantiate, how they reflect back on me and shape my moral character, how they cohere with my path in life, and so on. As agents, we are not merely causes of good and bad outcomes (as consequentialism supposes), nor are we simply arbitrary choosers (as autonomy theories suppose); rather, we are acting human subjects with a reasonably determinate nature who are responsible for our actions and for the development of our moral characters. This approach to ethics involves the following key themes.

First, actions are formed by the intentions of the agent. This is evident in the fact that we can only truly understand what someone is doing by taking up their perspective: it is not enough to observe a nurse remove life-support from a patient; we need to know whether the nurse is trying to end the patient's life or is removing an overly burdensome treatment. The nurse's intention is the critically necessary, though not sufficient, condition for accurately understanding what her action is. Until we know what an action is—and what intentions it embodies—we are in no position to evaluate it ethically.

Secondly, actions impact differently on agents and 'recipients'. My actions have good and bad effects on me, as well as various effects on others. It is the effect on me that is critical, for the meaning of my choice gives meaning to me as agent. Consider, for example, the difference between death as a result of murder and death as a result of an accident for which no one is responsible. In both cases the key outcome is the same—a person

13. See Chappell, *Understanding Human Goods*, Chapter 3.

dies—but in one case there is an agent responsible for that death, an agent whose intention and choice make him a murderer, and thereby make the person who dies a victim of crime. The specifically moral quality of the act, as murder rather than accident (or self-defence), derives from its primary impact on the agent (and thence on the victim). This is why, as Aristotle noted, we become virtuous or vicious people by acting in virtuous or vicious ways. In practice, *every* action is ethically significant, for every action impacts on the formation and stability of one's moral character, confirming a person in either virtue or vice.

Thirdly, this agent perspective draws our attention to the question of how, as 'acting subjects', we are related to the various goods we pursue in and through our actions. For example, any proposed comparison of the good of being alive with the bad of being disabled presupposes more fundamental questions about the way in which, as subjects, we are related to what is good or bad for us as human beings. What is it for something to be good or bad for me as an agent who must choose how to act in relation to that good or bad? As we will see, the critical issue is whether being alive is merely an *instrumental* good or is rather an *intrinsic* good for the person. In addressing this question our attention will be drawn, fourthly, to the question of what is it to be a human person, an acting subject for whom these goods are goods.

Understanding goods in relation to action

We return to our opening question, *Is it always good to be alive?* Fundamental differences between ways of approaching the question are now apparent. There is the perspective of a detached observer *thinking about* (comparing and contrasting) various states of affairs. There is the perspective of the conscious subject *choosing autonomously* on the basis of his or her experience of what is good or bad. There is the perspective of an *agent engaged with choices* about what *to do* in relation to the various goods of human existence. My central argument in this essay is that the agent's perspective cannot be reduced to either of the previous perspectives. That is, agency (and hence ethics) cannot be understood in terms of merely *thinking* about goods or *autonomously choosing* goods. Agency is rather about *engaging rationally* with goods that fulfil various aspects of our nature as human beings.[14] Human agents are faced with questions like these: Is be-

14. 'In order to be able to grasp the object of an act which specifies that act morally, it is

ing alive a good (for myself or for others) that I ought (always) to pursue and promote? Is being alive a good I may choose to sacrifice for the sake of other goods or in the name of personal autonomy? Is being alive a good I ought never 'attack' or destroy, even if it is not a good that I ought always to pursue?

In other words, there is a fundamental distinction between theory and practice: between, on the one hand, either *thinking* of life as *good* or bad or *experiencing* life as good or bad, and, on the other hand, *choosing* and *acting* so as to promote or to destroy life as a good or bad, for oneself or for another. Although acting cannot be reduced to thinking, *thinking* about the good of life has its place. In thinking of life as good for a person, we encounter our previous paradox: being alive (unlike being handsome or being intelligent or being famous) is not merely 'good for a person', since being alive is the presupposition for all other goods. Unless a person is (alive), he or she cannot have or experience other goods. As Aristotle and Aquinas reiterate, for living things, to be is to live: living things exist in virtue of living. Being alive is not a property added on to some already existing entity. A human corpse is what remains of a human being after death; it is not a human being minus life. The only human beings that exist are those that are alive. Of course, Aquinas also argued that in insofar as anything is (is alive), it is good.

Yet, there is clearly much more to the good of being a person than just being alive! The proper and distinctive *good of being a person* qua *person* involves rationality, self-consciousness, self-determination, and participation in a 'community of mutual recognition'.[15] Just being alive is the subordinate presupposition for these properly personal goods. This is why it may be right to lay down one's life either for another or for the sake of one's beliefs. Though being alive is a good presupposed in *being* a person, being alive is not the highest personal good. In refusing to deny one's beliefs, the martyr, like the hero rescuing a trapped person, may well lose his or her life in the course of an act of radical, personal self-determination. The martyr and the hero do not choose or seek death for its own sake, nor

---

therefore necessary to place oneself *in the perspective of the acting person.* The object of the act of willing is in fact a freely chosen kind of behaviour. To the extent that it is in conformity with the order of reason, it is the cause of the goodness of the will; it perfects us morally, and disposes us to recognise our ultimate end in the perfect good, primordial love'; John Paul II, *Veritatis Splendor,* # 78.

15. Robert Spaemann, *Persons—the Difference between 'Someone' and 'Something',* translated by Oliver O'Donovan (Oxford: OUP, 2006), 236.

as a means to their end. They simply accept death as a side-effect of doing what they must do in pursuit of their noble goals. This is why sadness at the death of the martyr or hero is tempered by admiration for *the person* he or she became in and through the actions that occasioned their death

That a person may willingly accept the loss of their life as a side-effect of *personal actions* in pursuit of higher goods is probably uncontroversial. The debated question today, however, is whether life may be deliberately ended as a means to purportedly higher, and more properly 'personal', ends. Those who argue that life may be directly taken as a means to an end in effect move from the correct observation that being alive is subordinate to (that is, *presupposed by*) the total good of the person, to the problematic claim that life may figure in our decision making as subordinate to (that is, *instrumental to*) the total good of the person.

It is easy to see why this move is tempting: if life is subordinate to higher personal goods, then when those higher goods seem absent, as for a persistently unconscious or gravely debilitated patient, being alive seems to have lost its 'instrumental' value, and seems no longer good for the person. Yet this move is problematic, for even if the life of the persistently unconscious person is no longer the foundation for higher goods, life retains its value as the basis of the person's very *being*. If I *as agent* treat life as merely an instrumental good, I thereby treat *the person* whose life it is as instrumental (to some purported good). Conversely, the most fundamental way of respecting a person, myself or others, is by respecting their life. Because all human values are instrumental toward, or constitutive of, the actualization of human nature in individual persons, these lives are the primary loci of value, and hence must be respected.[16]

In short, just because there is more to being a person than just being alive, it does not follow that we may treat being alive as merely instrumental to the good of the person.

The good of the person and goods for the person

For Thomas Aquinas, 'good' means perfection, fulfilment or completeness. Something is good if it is or is becoming all that it is to be. The good of the human person, therefore, consists in the fulfilment of a human being as the kind of being he or she properly is, namely, a free, self-determining

16. John Haldane, *Faithful Reason* (London: Routledge, 2004), 144.

subject.[17] There are many other aspects of human fulfilment—many goods *for* the person—but the good *of* a person as such is his or her fulfilment as a responsible, self-determining agent; it is a *moral* good that a person realises through the exercise of his or her freedom. This is why I spoke earlier about 'the person' a martyr or hero 'becomes' through their noble actions, even if this is at the expense of their lives. To become a martyr or a hero is to fulfil *one's being as a person* in a distinctive and noble way. This good or fulfilment of the person can only be realised through free action; it is a moral or practical good that cannot be reduced to 'natural' goods such as health, prosperity, or intelligence, and may well entail the loss of natural goods. Moreover, since persons are essentially relational beings, the good of the person is ultimately a good in relation to others: to God, loved ones and neighbours.

Because the good of the person as self-determining subject is more important than the good of being alive, the martyr and hero are free to lay down their lives for others. For the same reason, though not all are called to become martyrs or heroes, all human beings are summonsed to self-determination in relation to their death, summonsed 'to rise to the occasion' of their dying.[18] Unlike other animals, we know we will die, so we are unavoidably challenged to find and give meaning to our living and dying. One of the reasons why it is wrong to deliberately take life, one's own or that of another, is that killing puts an end to a person's self-determination. The practice of euthanasia, for example, involves accepting someone's decision today as his or her decision forever. To take life is to presume to finalise the meaning and value of a person's life. The fact that we cannot choose or control our birth or our parents is a reminder of what is always true of our being alive: it is a gift received, not a possession owned by 'a person' distinct from the living human being as such. To refuse ever to take life is to recognise the intrinsic value of every living person. Just as there is an existential contradiction in the idea of a person selling themselves into slavery, so there is an existential contradiction in the idea of a person making the final meaning-giving action of their lives to be one of ending their lives by suicide (whether 'physician assisted' or not). The person's life, which from their conception to that moment has been a life

17. In this section I draw on the work of Livio Melina, *Sharing Christ's Virtues*, translated by William E May (Washington, DC: CUA Press, 2001), Chapter 3.
18. The idea of 'rising to the occasion' of our dying was proposed in a lecture by ethicist William F May.

given, received and lived, suddenly becomes a life taken, controlled and ended.

Although ethical approaches that highlight personal autonomy are in keeping with this understanding of the good of the person, autonomy theories overlook the way in which a person's good is constituted in relation to the various goods of human nature. 'The good of the person is given its detailed content at the level of "goods for the person".'[19] Human actions are always directed towards some particular good that answers to human desires and inclinations. These goods, such as physical life and health, aesthetic enjoyment, sexual union and so on, are 'natural dimensions of the person in his unity of soul and body'.[20] As dimensions *of the person*, these inclinations, even those based in physical nature, are never merely 'animal' inclinations. Human beings are a unity of the physical and the spiritual: sexual desire, for example, is naturally directed towards another *person*, albeit as a bodily being.[21] Likewise, the desire to be healthy is a desire to be a healthy *person*, the desire to live is the desire to go on being the *person* one is. Because our inclinations towards the various goods that fulfil our nature are thoroughly personal, it takes effort and artifice to make them impersonal: for example, to make sexual desire casual or anonymous, or to regard one's life and health as merely biological.

In short, although human persons are not merely physical beings, they are persons in virtue of being the individual biological organisms they are. Human animality is the medium of personal realisation.[22] So it is a mistake to contrast what is good for me as a person with what is good for me as a biological organism, or to contrast personal life with physical life. The distinction between the *good of the person* as person and the various *goods for the person* is not an ontological dualism between (personal) freedom and (bodily) nature. The distinction between the good of the person and goods for the person rather affirms the primacy of the moral dimension 'that integrates within itself, in the originality of the practical perspective of love, goods intrinsic to the person respect for which is essential for the truth of love'.[23]

19. Melina, *Sharing Christ's Virtues,* 75.
20. Melina, 76.
21. See Roger Scruton, *Sexual Desire* (London; Weidenfeld and Nicholson, 1986), Chapter 4.
22. Spaemann, *Persons,* 240.
23. Melina, *Sharing Christ's Virtues,* 77.

In other words, a person's respect for him or herself, and for others, must include respect for the various natural goods that are intrinsically good for the person, above all the good of life. It makes no sense to claim that taking another's life could be good for the other as a person. If, as Aquinas held, the fundamental principle of moral reasoning is *do and pursue what is good and avoid evil*, then the good for self and others that I ought to pursue includes the natural goods intrinsic to human nature as a whole. An action is morally good if and only if it pursues what is good for the person while affirming the good of the person in all his or her totality.[24] Any direct attack on a good for the person will to some extent undermine the good of the person. Thus palliative care pursues a good for the person (relief of pain and other symptoms) in the context of the good of the person, whereas euthanasia not only destroys a good for person (life itself), but also thereby destroys the good of the person who ceases to be.

What is a human person?

These reflections cast further light on what it is to be a human person. *Person* is a term with a complex philosophical and theological history. *Person* does not pick out a natural category of beings, since it can apply to different kinds of beings (to humans, to angels, to God, but probably not to dolphins, and never to computers). Beings are said to be persons on the basis of possessing key properties such as rationality and self-consciousness, though these properties are possessed in different ways—divine 'rationality' is not the same as human rationality. Human persons are unique in that there is a sense in which humans 'become' persons, that is, become actively rational, self-conscious and responsible beings. Yet this fact should not mislead us into thinking that the unborn or the unconscious are not persons for, as Robert Spaemann has argued so eloquently, 'becoming' a person is not a transition from something to someone.[25] Thus, while it is true that children 'become persons' *because* they are recognised and accepted as persons, it is not recognition that makes the child a person, or

24. Melina, *Sharing Christ's Virtues*, 78. Biological life itself involves an organised totality, in which some aspects may need to be directly sacrificed for the good of the whole (for example, amputation of diseased limbs and organ donation). The sacrifice of biological part for biological whole may be ethically justified. The sacrifice of *biological* whole (life) for *personal* whole is not ethically justified, except as an unintended side-effect (as, for example, in the case of the martyr or hero).
25. In this section I draw on Spaemann, *Persons*, Chapter 18, 'Are All Human Beings Persons?'

co-opts the child into the world of persons. On the contrary, parents are always only recognising what their child already is (and is becoming): a person in their own right.

Thus, parents spontaneously treat their child *as* a person, not *as if* a person. When parents note that their child is 'becoming' a person, they are not responding to properties the child has suddenly acquired, but to properties that are emerging in the mutual reciprocity between parents and child. A child possesses capacities which may develop, but nothing develops into a person. Human persons are members of a natural kind, a living species whose instances are connected genealogically through biological reproduction. The human family is a community of persons from the outset. The severely disabled who may lack rationality and self-consciousness are still members of the human family; they are not a different kind of animal, they are patients, they are sick. They participate in the human family as recipients of physical and moral support.[26]

Conclusion

Just being alive is *always* good insofar as it is the most fundamental 'good for the person', even though being alive is not the most important good of human existence. There is more to what is good for me than just being alive, and in some circumstances I may rightly let go of life as I pursue more important goods, above all the specific 'good of the person' as a responsible, self-determining subject. That being alive is not the most important good does not entail that I may take life—whether my own or that of another—as a means to some good 'personal' end. To deliberately take a person's life is to attack the person whose life it is. There is thus an asymmetry in the ethical principles governing our actions in relation to life. On the one hand, being alive (unlike personal integrity) is not a good that must always be pursued; on the other hand, being alive is always a good that ought never be deliberately destroyed. Why the asymmetry? Why is it permissible to sacrifice one's life in pursuing the good of the person, but not permissible to take life in pursuing the good of the person?

The answer, I have argued, turns on the fact that the good of the person as 'autonomous' subject cannot be understood in isolation from the various goods for the person that constitute what it is to be a human being. There are goods more important than being alive, but the good of the

26. Spaemann, *Persons*, 244.

person cannot be divorced from those goods, above all, from the good of life. It is mark of wisdom to realise that staying alive should not be the most important value in my life; but it would be a mistake to treat my life as merely instrumental to my existence as a person. Respect for the life of a person is the most fundamental way of respecting the person whose life it is. That we respect each other as living persons is the ultimate basis for life together in society.[27]

27. I wish to thank Bernadette Tobin for helpful comments during the preparation of this essay.

Life's Endings: Mortality, Consequences, and the Principle of Double Effect

Helen McCabe

Helen McCabe
Plunkett Centre for Ethics, St Vincent Hospital,
Darlinghurst, Australia

Some people die all of a sudden; they leave us without warning and, most painfully, without 'saying goodbye'. They might be killed in motor vehicle accidents on their way home from work, or struck down by heart attacks while sitting at a desk, or suffer strokes while mowing the lawn. Other people—those who appear to flee from life—might drown accidentally, or fall from a cliff while rock-climbing. They are here one minute and, quite astonishingly, gone the next. If circumstances allow, an ambulance might be called and resuscitation measures commenced. But such efforts are not always successful, in which case our hapless fellows are unable to be rescued from the 'jaws of death'.

At other times, resuscitative efforts can be protracted so that a good while after oxygen has breathed life into a human body, cardiac function is restored and a ventilator forces lungs to breathe again. Some people whose lives are rescued in this way emerge from a coma with such profound brain injury that they appear to lack any kind of awareness at all. Instead, they exist in ways we cannot fully comprehend, their condition described as a 'persistent vegetative state' or, in Australian terms, a 'post-coma unresponsive state'. Some think we should continue to provide people caught in such a state with artificial nutrition and hydration. Others think that we should do no such thing.

Many more people are likely to die at the end of a protracted 'battle' with cancer or heart failure or, less commonly, Parkinson's disease, emphysema or some other form of chronic illness. The prolonged nature of these conditions is due just as often to the success of medical knowledge and know-how as it is to the normal course of the disease. Indeed, many people who suffer such conditions leave the world following the withdrawal of highly interventionist technologies, such as the life support machines we find in intensive care units. If those technologies which ventilate people's lungs and dialyse their kidneys and regulate their heart rates were to be continued indefinitely, their physiological life would continue, albeit in the highly-controlled confines of a hospital bed. However, in the long term we do not employ such means for the purpose of avoiding the fact of human mortality. Ordinarily, we know when it is time to let go, time to stop struggling, time to accept. Or, at least, we used to know.

Conversely, there are those who die after deliberately ingesting medically-prescribed medication; 'physician-assisted dying' (as this activity is termed) is thought, when practised, to ensure some kind of control over the terms and circumstances of one's death. Similarly, other people die after being administered lethal doses of medication by a medical or nursing practitioner. This practice known as euthanasia, while practically distinct from the former measure, is also concerned with seeking control over the timing and other circumstances of one's death. When people die in these ways, their passing has come to be described more often as an enactment of individual autonomy or choice and less commonly as killing. Notably, we now find increasing instances of these kinds of deaths even in those jurisdictions where such practices continue to be outlawed, where human life is still thought of as precious in some sense, or of inestimable worth or, in more religious terms, as sacred.

That life is sacred is a thought that has animated the health professions throughout history. From the time of Hippocrates in the fourth century BCE to the latter part of the twentieth century, physicians throughout the Western world have sworn to 'prescribe regimens for the good of my patients according to my ability and my judgment and never [to] do harm to anyone'. Further, they have sworn to refrain from giving 'a lethal drug to anyone if I am asked, nor . . . [to] advise such a plan'. That is, medical practitioners have not understood themselves to be in a position to determine who lives and who dies; nor has the law in Australia permitted them such an extraordinary power.

Some people now believe that the law should be changed to permit medical practitioners to directly bring about their patients' deaths (euthanasia) and/or to assist patients in ending their own lives (physician-assisted suicide). Those who argue for the legalisation of these measures generally draw on the ethical principle of respect for patient autonomy to justify their position. Accordingly, they understand human dignity in an attributive sense, as something that depends for its existence on an individual's possession of a particular notion of 'freedom', one that is expressed most often in acts of personal choice. Some of these voices believe that euthanasia ought to be granted legal sanction and, moreover, be included among other measures normally considered aspects of the practice of palliative care.[1] These voices seem to suggest that there is little difference, after all, between administering opiate analgesia to alleviate pain at the end of a person's life, and administering opiate analgesia *in order to* end someone's life. More concisely, they argue that as opiate analgesia administered to alleviate pain can, also, have the effect of shortening a person's life, there is no moral difference between those activities traditionally engaged in by palliative care professionals and those activities engaged in by those who administer euthanasia. In arguing in this way, they dismiss as 'sophistry'[2] the principle of double effect which has, over time, informed both the law and health care professions on these matters. Instead, they draw on those worldviews in which the right thing to do is to promote a particular consequence, such as the 'maximisation' of (some unspecified notion of) happiness or the 'maximisation' of individual preferences. On this view which we may call the 'post-traditional' worldview—the dominant worldview of contemporary Western societies—a particular activity or policy is justified if it promotes a particular desired consequence, such as preference satisfaction.

Another voice calls for a change in the law so as to safeguard medical practitioners against prosecution when faced with making what some believe to be a 'devil's choice' between, on the one hand, alleviating pain (with the possible effect of 'hastening death') or, on the other, with neglecting to treat a patient's pain. In proposing this particular argument, Roger Magnusson wants to provide a legal remedy for what he believes to be the dubious reliance on the principle of double effect, particularly

1. R Syme, *A Good Death: An Argument for Voluntary Euthanasia.* (Melbourne: Melbourne University Press, 2008), 227.
2. Syme, 115.

with regard to the distinction it makes between foresight and intention.[3] Similarly, Magnusson wants to protect medical practitioners from criminal liability when withdrawing (futile) life support treatment. To this end, he proposes that the law recognise a 'defence of necessity' which, if it were to be applied in such cases, would protect clinicians from the onus of criminal sanction should their patients die under such circumstances. Moreover, he argues, were such a defence accepted, it would reflect what Magnusson believes to be 'the true nature' of what is done when either narcotic analgesia is administered to the dying or when life support measures are withdrawn from those whose survival depends upon them. In other words, Magnusson proposes that the law's reliance upon the principle of double effect for determining the legal rectitude, or otherwise, of end-of-life decision making is questionable and ought to be replaced by a 'defence of necessity'.

In this essay, I will attempt to clarify and defend the use and meaning of the principle of double effect by addressing five things. First, I will sketch some key elements of the ethical tradition in which the principle of double effect finds its philosophical home. Secondly, I will attempt to demonstrate that this tradition takes seriously the moral psychology of the human person; hence, the importance of (among other things) the role of intention in moral deliberation. Thirdly, I will address the ways in which both the principle of double effect (PDE) and the tradition from which it is derived differ from a post traditional approach in which bioethical deliberation is, often enough, reduced to a consideration of some basic principles, especially the principle of respect for individual autonomy, and/or to a consideration of a particular consequence of human action. Fourthly, I will also consider the limits of the PDE in informing moral deliberation in end-of-life decision making, noting instead the way in which an often overlooked alternative 'ordinary/extraordinary means distinction' principle can be drawn from the same tradition to guide deliberation. Finally, I will conclude that the principle of double effect leaves a patient much less vulnerable in the face and force of modern medical practice than does a 'defence of necessity' or any other legal device.

3. R Magnusson, 'The Devil's Choice: Re-Thinking Law, Ethics and Symptom Relief in Palliative Care', in *Journal of Law, Medicine and Ethics*, 34/3 (2006): 559–69.

Key elements of traditional morality: the philosophical context of the principle of double effect

The PDE is drawn from (or reflects) a moral tradition, the terms of which are increasingly overlooked, misunderstood or simply dismissed in contemporary bioethical debate. Yet in order to understand the ethic that has traditionally informed end-of-life decision making, it is necessary to understand the following key elements of this approach.

First, traditional morality contains a complex set of prohibitions (such as on the use of torture), urgings (especially to care for others), obligations (to preserve human life, both one's own and that of others), rights (such as to freedom from slavery, servitude or persecution), and a range of virtues and vices. It is not reducible to a set of principles, for instance, nor can it be subsumed under a single overriding goal such as the 'maximisation of the greatest good'.

Secondly, it recognises that while consequences are morally significant, other things also matter, including the moral nature or '*moral kind*' of an act. For instance, injustice is understood as an act that is evil in itself beyond, simply, the consequences of injustice; it is possible, that is, to wrong someone even though they are unaware that they have been wronged. Traditional morality also recognises as significant the *intention* with which an act is performed (whether to alleviate pain or to end a person's life, whether to inflict pain or to cure an illness), the *motive* with which an act is performed (whether out of compassion or contempt), and the kind of person we become when we act in one way or another (a healer or a killer). In other words, it is a tradition which takes seriously a person's moral psychology or character.

Thirdly, traditional morality recognises that it is morally permissible to do something for the sake of a good purpose or objective (the relief of severe pain, for instance) even in the knowledge that the action may *also* bring about a bad result or bad 'side effect' (such as loss of consciousness or even the shortening of a person's life). What the tradition acknowledges, then, is that while moral agents ought always to avoid choosing and intending that which is evil, the human capacity to pursue that which is good is necessarily limited by the incapacity of human persons to avoid some evil side effects.[4] So, in the case of a seriously ill patient, it is permissible to seek the good end of pain relief even though the unintended bad

4. J Boyle, 'Medical Ethics and Double Effect: The Case of Terminal Sedation', in *Theoretical Medicine*, 8/4 (2004): 56.

end of a patient's earlier death is also another *distinct* possibility. At least, it is permissible in those cases where the means used to bring about good ends are not morally objectionable in themselves, as both means *and* ends matter. In other words, it is a tradition which prohibits any action that is evil in itself *even if* by engaging in such an act some kind of good outcome might be achieved. So, in distinction from some consequentialist worldviews, it would be considered morally illicit to intentionally kill someone in order to alleviate their pain, in the same way that it would be morally illicit to condemn an innocent person even if, by doing so, a violent uprising were averted. Conversely, there is nothing wrong *in itself* with administering analgesia, and there is nothing wrong either with withdrawing medical treatment which is futile for its proper purposes. It is these means, then, that are acceptable for achieving the good end of relief from pain and from the burden of futile and onerous treatment. Moreover, they are an acceptable means to bring about these good ends *even though* they may also bring about unintended bad ends.

Fourthly, it is a tradition which recognises that, in ethical reasoning, the good (such as health or pain relief) is to be considered prior to the right so that the right choice to make is that which assists in contributing to the good. In other words, knowing what is the right thing to do in any situation will depend, ultimately, on what moral purpose is at stake. For instance, the good of medical practice is health, healing and the alleviation of suffering associated with illness and injury. So, the right thing for a medical practitioner to do would be, on the one hand, to prescribe and perform those activities aimed at rescuing, restoring and maintaining health, and/or alleviating the symptoms associated with illness, disability and injury and, on the other hand, avoiding those activities which are either harmful to health and life or futile for their purposes, such as continuing advanced life support measures for a patient who has suffered 'brain death'.

Fifthly, traditional morality has always recognised that the obligation to preserve one's life has its limits. The so-called ordinary/extraordinary means distinction is a principle which rules that we ought to undertake any *ordinary* means of preserving our lives, such as crossing the road carefully or undergoing a surgical procedure should we develop appendicitis. At least these examples would count as 'ordinary' in a contemporary Western democracy. However, should the means to preserving our lives entail measures considered to be *extraordinary*, such as having to travel overseas to obtain treatment or to undergo treatment which is too painful to endure or psychologically repugnant, then the duty can be foregone. So, what is considered 'ordinary' (relative to time, place, economic circumstances and so forth) is also obligatory; what is considered 'extraordinary' (under particular personal, social and economic circumstances) is considered optional. That is, while both life and health are goods to be valued and promoted, they are not the ultimate end of human life; instead they are valued in relation to the final end or purpose of human living: the spiritual end.[5]

Admittedly, these various elements of traditional morality are controversial and require reasoned defence. However, this task will not occupy us here; instead, I will demonstrate how the PDE, in reflecting the elements of this tradition, guides end-of-life decision making in contemporary medical practice.

Doing good, alleviating pain and the principle of double effect

As already noted, some people think that there is no moral difference between a) administering narcotic analgesia to a dying person in order to alleviate severe pain which may, inadvertently, *also* have the effect of shortening that person's life and b) administering narcotic analgesia for the purpose of ending that person's life. However, to the extent that they believe this to be the case, they overlook what the PDE both recognises and seeks to protect.

According to this principle, narcotic analgesia may be administered for palliative purposes when the following requirements are met: a) the nature of the act must be good in itself (and alleviating pain is a good thing to do); b) the intention in administering narcotic analgesia is to alleviate pain and not to hasten death; c) the good effect of pain relief outweighs the bad effect of death in cases where the patient is seriously ill; and d) the good effect (pain relief) is not achieved by the bad effect (death);[6] that is, it would be morally wrong to intentionally end a patient's life in order to alleviate pain, even though pain relief is a legitimate purpose of both medicine and nursing. In this sense, palliative care ought always to be practised in accordance with the proper standards of this particular medi-

5. K O'Rourke, 'When to Withdraw Life Support?' in *The National Catholic Bioethics Quarterly*, 8/4 (2008): 666.
6. DF Kelly, *Contemporary Catholic Health Care Ethics* (Washington DC: Georgetown University Press, 2004).

cal specialty, as have been determined over years of experience in managing pain and other distressing symptoms.[7]

Should a person die in consequence of receiving properly prescribed and properly administered opiate medication, then that person's death is considered, according to the PDE, a 'bad side effect'. That is, the PDE holds that actions can reach a causal fork leading to two different (but morally significant) outcomes, one of which is intended (for example, pain relief) and one which is unintended (for example, respiratory depression, possibly leading to death). So, in the *unlikely* event that a person should die after receiving responsibly administered doses of morphine intended to alleviate pain, that person's death is not understood as causally connected in a *direct* sense. For this reason, it differs, morally-speaking, from the kind of act that follows from a direct intention to kill the person. Conversely, the character of what is intended, should it be bad, such as killing, is neither justified by the PDE nor does it find appeasement in any good motive, such as compassion; those who argue for a legitimate right to receive euthanasia sometimes attempt to justify the measure in this way. However, on a traditional view, neither good nor bad motives alter the actual moral character of what is intended, or chosen.

Nonetheless, motives do play a significant role in determining *the kind of person* we become when we act under their influence. For instance, we might do that which is good and right by a person who is dying because we are motivated by compassion, empathy and fellow-feeling. However, we might also do what is good and right by a dying person because we are motivated by fear of litigation. While in both cases we do that which is good and right, our moral characters are altered by the motivations with which we act. In influencing our moral characters, motives (like virtues) also determine the degree to which we can be relied upon to do one thing or another; for instance, the sufficiently virtuous medical practitioner can be relied upon to protect the interests of patients whereas the practitioner who acts out of a fear of litigation may be less reliable in doing so in such circumstances where, for instance, nobody witnesses his/her neglect, or where the patient is thought unlikely to sue. In this way, motives have an

7. See C Faull, Y Carter, and L Daniels, *Handbook of Palliative Care* (Massachusetts: Blackwell Publishing, second edition 2005); also Scottish Intercollegiate Guidelines Network (2009). Control of Pain in Patients with Cancer. Retrieved 28 January, 2009, from http://www.sign.ac.uk/pdf/SIGN106.pdf

important role to play in moral deliberation.[8] Nonetheless, they do not alter the character of other aspects of moral deliberation, such as intention

If an intention is bad in itself (such as to kill one's patients), then the action which follows this intention is also morally wrong, even if motivated by compassion and concern. Indeed, if a medical practitioner intends to kill a patient, even if the intention goes unfulfilled (for example, no opportunity arises to administer a lethal dose of medication) it remains bad nonetheless and the moral character of the doctor is adversely affected. That is, while the same practitioner would escape a criminal charge, he or she would be held, on a traditional view, *morally* culpable nonetheless. Also, if the practitioner acts in the *belief* that she or he is killing a patient then the practitioner does what is morally wrong even if the belief itself is inaccurate (for example, the dose of morphine prescribed is insufficient to cause death) and, in the absence of any suspicion of criminal intent, even though the law would not find a case against that practitioner (given that the patient has not, in fact, died).

Similarly, if practitioners act on the belief that they are alleviating pain and there is no intention to cause death, they do nothing wrong, morally-speaking, should the patient die unless they act incompetently, for instance, by negligent prescription of opiates and sedation in doses that are disproportionate to the pain and/or agitation suffered.[9] Should practitioners prescribe opiates and sedation incompetently, they are rightly considered both morally and legally negligent. For this reason, we might want to consider placing conditions on (or even repealing) their licences to practice. Nonetheless, it would be stretching the point to describe those same practitioners, incompetent though they might be, as actual killers or murderers in the absence of a finding of an intention to kill the patient. A finding of negligence is not morally equivalent to a finding of murder. Yet, this is what is often implied in a post traditional world.

In that same world, we also discover the belief that withdrawing or withholding life support measures, such as withdrawing a ventilator from a patient who is unlikely to be able to breathe independently of it, is equiv-

---

8. L Trinkaus Zagzebski, *Virtues of the Mind: An Inquiry into the Nature of Virtue and the Ethical Foundations of Knowledge* (Cambridge: Cambridge University Press, 1996), 131–34.
9. See, for example, World Health Organisation (2008). WHO's Pain Ladder. Retrieved 12 November, 2008, from http://www.who.int/cancer/ palliative/painladder /en, and Faull, Carter, and Daniels, *Handbook of Palliative Care*, 2005.

alent to killing the patient.[10] However, on a traditional view, the continued use of life support technology when health cannot be restored is not morally equivalent to killing the patient. Indeed, the act of withdrawing medical treatment is complete when the treatment is withdrawn (as intended) and not when the patient dies if that is, ultimately, the (unintended) outcome. That is, the intention is realised when the treatment is withdrawn; the patient's death is a morally distinct event, the cause of which is attributed to the patient's underlying pathology, such as cardiac or respiratory failure. By way of illustrating the point, it is possible to demonstrate that, in the most unlikely event that a healthy person should have life support technology imposed upon them, the removal of such measures would not bring about the death of that person, given that they do not already suffer from a life threatening condition in the first place. The withdrawal of treatment that is medically futile is not, then, equivalent to killing a patient. Rather, it is humbly to recognise the moral, practical, psychological, intellectual, economic, and spiritual limits of medical practice. Moreover, the decision to withdraw medically futile treatment is based on the value of the *treatment*, and not on the value of a patient's life.

To argue that the withdrawal of futile treatment is morally equivalent to killing the patient is to conflate intention with ability to foresee, which are two morally and psychologically distinct notions. It is also to dismiss from consideration the kind of act that is engaged in. To simply look to the outcome of an action, determine whether it could be foreseen and then rule on its moral status excludes from view the moral character of the action, the intention with which the activity is engaged in, the motivation for performing the action, as well as any other possible or actual consequences of that same action, such as the prolongation of suffering or the raising of false hopes.

On a traditional worldview, when medical treatment is no longer able to restore a patient to health, when treatment becomes futile, the medical practitioner may (and should) withdraw or withhold that treatment even though it can be foreseen that, in doing so, a patient may die as a side effect of that otherwise morally legitimate decision (given that the treatment can forestall the patient's death). By way of comparison, it is possible to argue that we are justified in building, for instance, a sporting arena *for the sake of* promoting health in a community, even though we can foresee that some people will suffer sporting injuries as a side effect of that deci-

10. Magnusson, 'The Devil's Choice', 563.

sion. Or we might be justified in building new roads to facilitate transport services even though we can foresee that some people will suffer injuries or even be killed in consequence of using those roads. That people are injured or killed as a consequence of using those services does not mean that those who decided to build sporting arenas and roads are complicit in maiming and killing people: this was not their intention.

Yet, post traditionalists argue that, given the outcome, medical practitioners engaged in activities which inadvertently shorten patients' lives ought to be held morally accountable for the deaths of their patients.[11] At least, in recent times, we can find such pronouncements nestled subtly in among calls for the legalisation of euthanasia. However, if a medical practitioner is to be held responsible for ending a patient's life under such circumstances (for example, by withdrawing life support technology and alleviating severe pain at the end of a patient's life), then the practitioner must already possess an obligation to keep patients alive at all times, under all circumstances, for all reasons and for none, as well as *forever* or at least until, presumably, the patient requests to be allowed to die or be killed. But the practitioner bears no such obligation; it is not practically, intellectually, financially or in other ways reasonably possible to sustain life indefinitely.

Avoiding harm, withdrawing or withholding treatment, and the 'ordinary/extraordinary means distinction' principle

The PDE rules that the patient's obligation to preserve his or her life arises only when available treatment offers some hope of benefit and with some degree of duration.[12] This principle assists in guiding most decisions concerned with end-of-life matters. However, not *all* end-of-life decision making can be guided coherently by the PDE. For instance, the withdrawal of artificial nutrition and hydration from the patient in a so-called 'post-coma unresponsive state' cannot be justified by the provisions of the PDE as such measures are neither overly-burdensome to the patient (as the patient is—as far as can be known—insensate), nor futile for its purposes (artificial mixtures of 'food' or chemical nutrients and the technical delivery of hydration *do* fulfil their purpose of nourishing and hydrating the patient). For this reason, those who rely singularly upon the PDE to

11. Magnusson, 564.
12. M Panicola, 'Catholic Teaching on Prolonging Life: Setting the Record Straight', in *The Hastings Center Report*, 31/6 (2001): 14–25.

guide deliberation in caring for patients in post-coma unresponsive states must conclude that, in the absence of 'very strong reasons against it in a particular case', artificial nutrition and hydration should always be provided.[13]

Others, however, have looked within the same tradition to find another principle for guiding moral deliberation in such cases: the 'ordinary/extraordinary means distinction' principle. This principle is sometimes conflated with the PDE but to the extent that it is, the tradition from which it emerges is misinterpreted. The older 'ordinary/extraordinary means distinction' principle requires medical practitioners to act so as to preserve life except in those cases where to do so would take the patient beyond the realm of what is possible for that particular patient to do, or bear, under the circumstances. Significantly, the tradition is patient-focused. Indeed, according to the ordinary/extraordinary means distinction principle, the patient's obligation to conserve his or her life arises only when available medical treatment is not too painful, when it is reasonably accessible, when it does not denigrate or, in other ways, cause psychological suffering to the patient (such as by its repugnance), and when it does not violate the patient's moral and/or spiritual well-being, for instance, a blood transfusion in the case of someone who is a member of the Jehovah's Witness faith. Of course, what is considered ordinary for some people may be extraordinary for others. Much depends upon the culture, economy, time, place and other material, psychological and spiritual circumstances of a person's life, including the resources of others to provide for care and medical treatment.

What distinguishes the 'ordinary/extraordinary means distinction' from the PDE is that it takes into account not only the burdens of treatment but, also, the burden(s) of the patient's actual *condition*.[14] For instance, should a reasonable patient be severely distressed by the difficulties of living with end-stage muscular dystrophy or with end-stage motor neurone disease, that patient would not be required to seek every possible medical means for prolonging life, such as taking antibiotics to treat an episode of pneumonia. Or, should a patient in a 'post-coma unresponsive state' refuse (by means of an advance directive or through their proxy) artificial nutrition and hydration on the grounds that it is an extraordinary means of care under the circumstances (the prolongation of a severely

13. A Fisher, 'The Ethics of Care for Those with Post-coma Unresponsiveness and Related Conditions', in *Bioethics Outlook*, 16/2 (2005): 5.
14. See D Sulmasy, 'End of Life Care Revisited', in *Health Progress*, 87/4 (2006): 51.

incapacitated life when even the slightest recovery is most unlikely), then medical and nursing practitioners may and should withhold the relevant measures. That is, it is morally legitimate to withdraw or withhold health care measures that will not, for instance, restore the patient's health or restore consciousness.[15] And it is morally legitimate to withhold these same measures so as not to prolong the suffering a patient might endure in consequence of living with their actual affliction. As artificial nutrition and hydration simply acts to prolong physiological life in a permanently post-comatose patient without, at the same time, offering any hope of recovery or even improvement, then the patient may forego such measures. It is in considering these matters, then, that the obligation to persist with medical treatment finds its reasonable limits and thereby fosters the instinct to preserve life on the part of medical practitioners without, at the same time, demanding medical practice that is overly-zealous and unreasonable.

To acknowledge that the 'ordinary/extraordinary means distinction' principle sets limits on the extent to which medical treatment is to be provided is not to say that the traditional worldview admits of differences in the value of the lives of human persons. On the contrary, it holds that human persons, *without exception*, possess an innate or intrinsic dignity by virtue of their humanity. Thus, the tradition rejects the thought that the value of a person's life is based in such arbitrary qualities as health status, consciousness, age, social standing, or quality of life measures. It also rejects the thought that there is such a thing as 'a life unworthy of life'. Moreover, it rejects the utilitarian view, as outlined and dismissed by Kleinig, that the value of a life is measured by its 'worth or usefulness to others'.[16] Rather, it insists on upholding the principle of the sanctity of every human person. However, it does not follow from this that human life must be preserved at all times, by all means, at all costs, and under all circumstances; there are practical, moral, psychological and spiritual limits to the preservation of human lives. Further, the sanctity of life principle, in requiring utmost respect for human life, should not be deployed to justify the application of medical technology for *its* own sake. Simply because we have the technological means for prolonging life indefinitely does not mean, *ipso facto*, that we must always and in every case harness

15. Panicola, 'Catholic Teaching on Prolonging Life', 22.
16. J Kleinig, *Valuing Life* (Princeton: Princeton University Press, 1991), 216.

its powers. Indeed, to do so is to invert the proper purpose of medical practice to its means.

Moral character and human dignity

Post traditionalists want to dismiss the PDE as irrelevant, instead insisting that when a patient dies a doctor must be responsible for that death. Or they propose, at least, that end-of-life decision making characteristically involves medical practitioners in making 'devil's choices'. Specifically, post traditionalists tend to constrain the ethical focus to a concern over a particular outcome. For this reason, by ignoring a range of other ethical considerations, they are able to conclude that, if it is ethically and legally permissible to do such things as withdraw life support measures even while knowing that the patient may die soon afterwards, there should be no complaint if euthanasia and physician-assisted suicide (PAS) are adopted as an integral part of palliative care practice.[17]They further argue that legitimate access to such measures has the effect of increasing choices that patients have, and that this factor alone is ethically desirable. Underlying *this* thought is an understanding of human dignity that, as distinct from the traditional worldview, is contingent or detachable: something that is extrinsic to a human person.

Human dignity is now most often viewed as something that is lost when people age, become ill, lose their reason or consciousness, 'lose control' or become dependent upon others to help them do such things as mobilise or eat or bathe. Human dignity, in other words, is something that can in some sense be taken away or extinguished. Contemporary debate about 'dying with dignity' reflects of this understanding. The notion of human dignity also underlies that of human rights and, for this reason, is often employed as a legal or semi-legal term. At the same time, in ways that are intertwined, human dignity is an idea increasingly paired (if not conflated) with that of individual 'interest' and/or individual will or choice relative to that interest.[18] Thus, the terms of debate over the legalisation of euthanasia are couched in the language of dignity, rights, autonomy, and will or choice. We hear, for instance, that those who are dying and are denied the 'right to die' (by which is meant the 'right' to have their choice to

---

17. See R Syme, *A Good Death*, 227.
18. YM Barilan and M Brusa, 'Human Rights and Bioethics', in *Journal of Medical Ethics*, 34/4 (2008): 383.

be administered euthanasia 'respected') must, therefore, die in such a way that is considered by some to be 'undignified'. Moreover, we hear that a good society would provide the dying with euthanasia should they choose it for themselves because a good society, it is said, is one in which an individual's autonomy or choice for one thing or another is 'respected'. Indeed, respect for individual autonomy or choice is now discussed *as if* it carries the same moral weight as does the Kantian idea of respect for a person.[19] Accordingly, medical and nursing practitioners are called upon to respect the choices of their patients irrespective of the nature of those choices, including that of euthanasia.

However, on this post traditional worldview, it is the choices of conscious and rational patients *only* that must be respected. Indeed, those medical and nursing practitioners who would choose *not* to be implicated in providing such measures as euthanasia would not have *their* choice respected. Instead, those who object to any proposal to legalise the deliberate ending of a patient's life are derided as delusional (post traditionalists believe they are ending their patients' lives anyhow) and immoral (for failing to respect patients' autonomy).[20] This inconsistency, if it is acknowledged at all, is glossed over by those who think that the purpose of medical practice is, simply, to respect the autonomous choices of patients. For instance, Syme states that 'it is a mistake to focus on the intention of the doctor in this debate—he [sic] is secondary to the wishes and intentions of the person he is guiding in treatment.'[21]

Not everyone would agree. For instance, their support for euthanasia notwithstanding, nurses practising in Belgium where euthanasia is legally available have objected that doctors, in prescribing euthanasia, often fail to engage them in prior consultation. That is, in Belgium, while consultation with nurses is legally required prior to performing euthanasia, and while they are deeply implicated in providing for this measure, nurses are consulted as to its 'appropriateness' in only fifty-seven per cent of cases.[22] The nurses' objection concerns a failure on the part of doctors to respect their autonomy. At the same time, we can look to those same national

19. T Lysaught, 'Respect. Or, How Respect for Persons Became Respect for Autonomy, in *Journal of Medicine and Philosophy*, 29/6 (2004): 676.
20. R Syme, *A Good Death*, 15.
21. Syme, 28.
22. M Berghs, B Dierckx de Casterle, and C Gastmans, 'The Complexity of Nurses' Attitudes toward Euthanasia: a Review of the Literature', in *Journal of Medical Ethics*, 31/8 (2005): 441–6.

contexts where euthanasia and PAS are considered aspects of end-of-life decision making to see that those patients whose reason is impaired in some way are consequently vulnerable to being administered euthanasia whether or not they have or would have made such a choice. For instance, in Belgium, we find in one study that euthanasia has been provided in the absence of a patient's request for the measure because those who administered the lethal dose believed the relevant patients to be 'too ill to consent'.[23] The inconsistencies in this post traditional worldview are all too obvious.

In conclusion

On a traditional view, killing is wrong in itself. Hence, it cannot be made right by either an act of consent or a change in the law. On the same view, the moral character of those who profess to cure and to heal is granted great significance, given the moral nature of the work engaged in and the vulnerability of those in need of health care. To the extent that a post traditional view dismisses as irrelevant the significance of the clinician's moral character, to that extent it dismisses what ensures the safety and well-being of the patient to a far greater extent than a retrospectively applied 'defence of necessity' or any other legal device. Indeed, should the importance of a clinician's moral character be disregarded altogether, we are left wondering on what grounds we would, were we to become ill, rely on that clinician to uphold our interests, to protect and promote our health, or even to respect our autonomy. And this should worry us greatly.

---

23. J Bilsen, R Vander Stichele, F Mortier, and L Deliens, 'Involvement of Nurses in Physician-Assisted Dying', in *Journal of Advanced Nursing*, 47/6 (2004): 583–91.

Interface Vol 13 1&2/2010

Beginning and Ending of Life: A Personal Journey

Michael Kain

Michael Kain
Adelaide, Australia

The following does not aim to be a contribution to the academic debate of issues discussed in this volume. It is an anecdotal memoir and personal reflection on life issues as they affected me when I was a medical student, a young doctor in the sixties, and in my subsequent medical practice.

Background

Born in 1941, I began studying medicine at Adelaide University in 1959, and became a general practitioner. I still practice in Adelaide and have enjoyed medical work for over forty years, with a special interest in palliative care for at least twenty-five years

I am also a Roman Catholic layperson, which has quite some bearing on what I write here, so please bear with me in the next few paragraphs until I get to the issues I wish to discuss. I would not class myself as a perfect Catholic as I do not always agree with everything the Church says, but it is a way of life that suits me. Catholicism in the sixties was somewhat stricter than it is now.

The challenges of Vatican II

The Second Vatican Council in 1962 brought spiritual renewal and a reconsideration of the Church's place in the modern world. It also brought liturgical reform, giving the laity fuller participation in the liturgy. This meant, for example, that parish councils were to be involved in the running of the parishes.

This was actually a very big change in the way that Catholics were to consider the Church. It caused problems for some priests, who found the changes very difficult to accept (it seemed that Father no longer knew best!), and many lay people found (and still find) difficulty with the changes. For example, the Latin Mass is still wanted by a minority, as is a full return to the authority of the priest.

Did this affect me personally?

In retrospect, I feel that it did. My mother was a good Catholic woman who instilled the sound precepts of the Church in all her children. To later feel that I could question some of them was a new experience for me, although I have never felt the need to overturn many of my mother's lessons—can any of us really do this?

In time I have come to feel a bit differently about a number of medical issues at which I will now look.

Sex and Contraception

In the sixties, in the groups in which I moved, extra-marital sex was not overtly practised. There did not appear to be a great deal of 'begetting', as the Bible puts it. Of course it did go on, but was frowned upon. Abortions were performed (more of which later). Sudden 'shotgun' marriages did occur, or young women disappeared to other states to have their illegitimate children and adopt them out. St Joseph's Home for unmarried women run by the Daughters of Charity at Fullarton was an organisation in Adelaide set up to look after these women, who largely came from interstate. They had their babies and then returned home without them.

Sex and marriage did actually 'go together like a horse and carriage', as the popular song at the time said (although 'love' was mentioned rather than 'sex'). An acquaintance said to me recently, with a slightly wry grin, that the main reason he and his wife married was to have sex.

Most of my friends at the time were married by the time they were twenty or twenty-one. Helen and I were considered on the shelf by the time we were married at 24!

Everybody in society, Catholic and non-Catholic, frowned upon sex and pregnancy outside of marriage.

Enter 'the pill'

With the arrival of the pill, contraception was available in a new form that was easy to administer and that allowed sexual activity without fear of pregnancy.

No preparation was required before intercourse. Furthermore, it was far more effective than any other contraceptive at the time. This should have made its acceptance easy, but that was not immediately the case. It actually took a while before many medicos could accept it.

In 1961, Schering introduced into Australia the pill called Anovlar. This had an enormous social impact. Women's liberation groups felt that this was, at last, a way to throw off the shackles of male domination Later they could accuse males of ruining the health of women when side effects became obvious!

The encyclical *Humanae Vitae* issued by Pope Paul VI caused controversy since it reaffirmed the position of the Church against contraception in any form. This did not help to solve the problems that now came to the fore in Catholic communities. Many objected to the Church not allowing contraception and ultimately ignored the encyclical. Others strongly supported it. Many in the Church found *Humanae Vitae* confusing because they felt it went against the advice of the International Commission that had been set up by the Vatican.

I attended many Catholic discussion groups but was not sure in my own mind whether I as a doctor could support a ban on the pill. One of the conclusions reached was that Catholic doctors could prescribe the pill to women provided that they were married and not Catholic! Whilst this may appear silly now, remember that this was the sixties and life was different then. One of the points raised in the debate was that the pill would change sexual behaviour, and in time it certainly did that.

The rest, as they say, is history; contraception in many forms is now an accepted part of our lives. As stated above, I participated in many discussions on this issue as a young doctor, and became very involved in providing pre-marriage courses (known in those days as Pre Cana courses), helping to teach the Billings method of family planning in Adelaide. I also helped to set up this program in Mount Gambier—one that still exists in the Mount. This method of family planning is allowed by the Church and helped many Catholics who felt they could not take the pill. It is not perfect and has its own problems but has been good for many couples.

There were many tensions at the time as to what we young doctors should or could do. After much thought I felt that I had to exercise my own conscience here. The Church now does allow the use of *informed* conscience in difficult matters. There was and still is some confusion about the role of conscience in the Church, which continues to cause difficulties for many.

I came to feel that I could not really refuse to prescribe the pill if indicated. (Incidentally, if I did refuse to prescribe, I was obliged to find a doctor who would do so.) I prescribed it to those who asked and had no contra-indications. I did not feel I could force ideas on people who did not feel the same way as the Church. Women worn out with bearing and tending many children, those with financial problems, women with medical problems, husbands who were banished to the sleep-out, young women who were really trying to avoid conception, and so on, presented me with a whole range of people who were grateful for the help that the pill gave. In the final analysis, however, I had more problems with side effects than with whether I should prescribe it or not—the dose of the pill in those days was extremely high compared to present dosages.

I feel my response to the many problems faced at the time was reasonable and have not regretted it.

Abortion

One would have thought that easier contraception would have meant a decline in the number of abortions. If this was the case, it did not appear obvious in general practice.

One half of the young women in my practice appeared to be trying hard to become pregnant and the other half were trying desperately not to do so. Neither side appeared to be winning!

In 1969 legislation was enacted in South Australia that liberalised the abortion law. Prior to this time, abortion was largely illegal, the main recourse being to backyard procedures or to interstate travel. There are, of course, no accurate figures on the number of illegal abortions carried out before the above legislation, but it is thought perhaps to have been much the same as after the change in legislation.

As a young doctor I did not see many who had undergone a backyard abortion, or did not know if any had done so. I do remember two women who were ill with pelvic infection but who recovered. At this time a doctor acquaintance was struck off for performing abortions. Even after the liberalisation of the law it was still not easy to obtain an abortion—at least for a short time.

'Safeguards' were introduced. The conditions that had to be met for legal abortion were either

1. that the continuation of the pregnancy would be detrimental to the mother's physical or emotional health or
2. the child would be physically or mentally handicapped.

In either case, *two doctors* had to assess the situation and sign legal documents.

This, again, presented me with a moral dilemma. I could not really approve of abortion and I had difficulty in signing the second form; my conscience would not allow me to do so. Fortunately, the other doctors to whom I sent the patients were understanding of my position and did not request me to proceed.

This may seem like dodging the issue and it probably was. However, I was (and remain) sympathetic to these women. They were my patients, and many needed a lot of help for such things as depression and feelings of guilt following the termination of a pregnancy. This became my major role in the terminations that were carried out in those days.

Foetal abnormalities

Whilst I have stated I do not personally approve of abortions, I cannot say that I am not unmoved by many requests where foetal abnormality is the problem and there is no chance that the child will survive for long after birth, for example, in cases of anencephaly (lack of brain development), hydrocephaly or multiple foetal abnormalities.

I must confess that I often cannot see any point in continuing with these tragedies. I am aware that any human life is sacred but, as the foetus will not live a life to any extent, I cannot feel sad at the discontinuation of most of these pregnancies. (I hasten to add that these are *my* thoughts, not those of my Church; I am here exercising my personal conscience, although I have never acted on it to discontinue a pregnancy.) Actually, the medical profession has become quite adept at diagnosing conditions such as spina bifida and Down's syndrome before birth; in most cases, probably, the abnormal foetus, when discovered, is aborted.

My feelings here are mixed. These foetuses *can* survive and I have a few patients who have lived productive lives with these conditions. I have delivered a couple who are doing well. Abortion does not seem ethical. However, I am not the parent of one of these children, and I am not totally unsympathetic when an unhappy decision to abort is made.

Again, my role is often that of support after the event. To finish this question of abortion, the legislation has not changed but I now send my patients to hospital where the termination is carried out. They are usually seen by a social worker who arranges the termination with the doctor after some counseling which is usually supportive of termination. I have not seen a patient refused an abortion for at least thirty years. One might facetiously observe that the only prerequisite for termination of pregnancy these days is that one must be pregnant!

This comment is not meant to be flippant. It is meant to show how the performance of abortion has changed since the early days of the change in legislation, and also to point out that 'safeguards' put into legislation do not really hold out for long; they generally appear to be ignored after a short interval.

Euthanasia

This is 'a happy death'; '80% of Australians are in favour of euthanasia'; '70% of doctors admit to mercy deaths'. These are the sort of headlines that have been around for years and appear to be gaining some momentum, especially since the Netherlands have made it legal to euthanase people (more of which later).

In the sixties, there was not a great deal of discussion of euthanasia among the doctors with whom I mixed: it was illegal, it was killing and we were on a mission to keep people alive rather than kill them. I realise that this was a simplistic view, but that was then.

What is euthanasia?

Euthanasia is the *active* killing of an individual to relieve their suffering. To make the issue clearer it is perhaps better to start with what euthanasia is *not*.

- It is *not* allowing nature to take its course. A dying person does not have to eat or drink if they do not want to do so.

- It is *not* stopping life support when this is no longer appropriate (a difficult choice that relatives often have to face).
- It is *not* giving heavy doses of a drug which is necessary to relieve pain, knowing that the drug could shorten the patient's life. This is known as the 'principle of double effect', where the intention is to relieve suffering *not* to kill the patient.

This last case is already covered in law. I strongly suspect that the 70% of doctors who admit to mercy killing fall into this category. I recognise that there is sometimes a thin line here but the difference **is** important; I speak from twenty-five years of experience in palliative care.

Has euthanasia been asked of me? Yes, but usually by the relatives. I recognise their suffering as well as that of the patients, but I am unable to comply with their request.

Last year I was asked by a patient to consider euthanasia when his time came. When that time arrived he used every means in his power to stay alive— and ruefully admitted that to me.

Would I consider administering euthanasia?

I have never done so but during the AIDS epidemic I saw many cases of the full-blown disease**, a** truly awful condition. I sometimes wondered whether I could always stick to my principles if faced with this on a continuous basis. I must admit feeling relief when the sufferers in question died.

Does Palliative care have all the answers?

No, but we are a lot better at it than we once were. We cannot always relieve pain but heavy sedation does help. I realise that this could be construed as a slow euthanasia, but I stand by the principle of double effect.

The Netherlands experience

In 2002 the Netherlands allowed doctors to kill patients if they followed certain guidelines.

- The patient must be experiencing unbearable pain
- The patient must be conscious
- The request must be voluntary

- Euthanasia alternatives must be considered
- The patient's death cannot inflict suffering on others
- There must be more than one person involved in making the decision
- Only a doctor can euthanase a patient

It is my understanding that all these provisions turned out to be wishful thinking and, as with abortion, the rules are not always followed. The guidelines have been broadened to include the killing of children under the age of twelve. Intervention to terminate a life is now allowed *without an express request.*

This regulation was brought in to allow euthanasia for those who cannot ask for it (for example, psychiatric patients and handicapped newborn babies). Doctors make the judgment as to whether the child or person has a reasonable quality of life. There is now a movement in Holland to allow people over the age of seventy to be killed if they are simply tired of life. This opens another can of worms. I have heard that the woman who introduced the euthanasia legislation now has some regrets; she feels that it was introduced far too early and that the rights of people who want to die naturally are being overlooked (there are, apparently, people who carry cards in their wallets saying they do not wish to be euthanased).

There are many factors that can be debated with respect to this issue. I hear politicians saying euthanasia will be well regulated and there will be no 'slippery slope' into bad practices. But why would our experience be any different from that in the Netherlands and what would stop the slide as it occurred with abortion?

These are the thoughts of a once young and now not so young doctor who has been through some interesting changes in thinking as far as medical life-issues are concerned. I do not pretend to know all the answers and am well aware that others will disagree with some of my thoughts. They are welcome to their thinking on these issues; these are *my* thoughts and feelings due to the way my life has been shaped.

It has been an interesting medical life and I am very grateful for having lived in these times.

List of Contributors

Professor Annette Braunack-Mayer is the Acting Head of the School of Population Health and Clinical Practice, The University of Adelaide, South Australia.

Dr Drew Carter, is a postdoctoral Research Fellow (Ethics), and Professor Annette Braunack-Mayer the Acting Head of the School of Population Health and Clinical Practice, The University of Adelaide, South Australia.

Dr Gerald Glesson is at Catholic Institute of Sydney, Sydney.

Associate Professor Rosalie Hudson is Honorary Senior Fellow in the School of Nursing & Social Work, at the University of Melbourne, and a consultant/ educator in aged care, palliative care and pastoral care.

Professor Gareth Jones, Anatomy Department and Structural Biology, University of Otago, Dunedin, New Zealand.

Dr Michael Kain is a General Practicioner, Adelaide

Dr Ian Maddocks is Emeritus professor of Palliative Care, Flinders University, Adelaide

Dr Helen McCabe is at the Plunkett Centre for Ethics, St Vincent Hospital, Darlinghurst NSW.

Dr Ea Mulligan is a Research Associate in the School of Law at Flinders University of South Australia.

Dr Gregory K Pike is Director of the Southern Cross Bioethics Institute, North Plympton, South Australia.

Bernadette Richards, BA, Dip Ed, LLB (Hons) is a Senior Lecturer in Law at the Law School, University of Adelaide.

Dr Margie Ripper is Associate Professor, Discipline of Gender Studies and Labour Studies in the School of Social Sciences at the University of Adelaide.